The Faith
That
Moves Mountains

Translated from the French
Original Title:
LA FOI QUI
TRANSPORTE LES MONTAGNES

Omraam Mikhaël Aïvanhov

The Faith
That
Moves Mountains

Izvor Collection — No. 238

P R O S V E T A

Canadian Cataloguing in Publication Data

Aïvanhov, Omraam Mikhaël, 1900-1986
    The faith that moves mountains

(Izvor collection ; no. 238)
Translation of: La foi qui transporte les montagnes.
ISBN 1-895978-25-4

    1. Faith. I. Title. II. Series: Izvor collection
(North Hatley, Quebec) ; no. 238.

BP610.A3513313 2000   299'.93   C00-901595-7

Prosveta Inc.
3950, Albert Mines, North Hatley, QC, Canada J0B 2C0

Readers are asked to note that Omraam Mikhaël Aïvanhov's teaching was exclusively oral. This volume includes passages from several different lectures all dealing with the same theme.

TABLE OF CONTENTS

1

FAITH, HOPE AND LOVE

But the intellect is the faculty that leads man to consider himself the lord of the world to the point where he defies God. It is that senseless pride that led some of the angels to defy God, and it is this that the devil hoped to awaken in Jesus.

Jesus resisted each of the temptations offered by the devil, because he had learned to master his physical body (against the temptation of physical food he set spiritual food), his astral body (he refused to put God's love to the test in vain), and his mental body (he refused to consider himself God's equal and chose to remain his servant).

It is very important to understand the meaning of the three temptations to which Jesus was exposed, because we too have to confront them in our everyday lives, and if we want to make progress in our inner life, we must begin by seeing all this very clearly. The importance of clear-sightedness becomes evident when we see that this episode is at the beginning of the Gospel. Jesus had just been baptized by John the Baptist in the Jordan; he had not yet chosen his first disciples or begun to teach. Those who want to put themselves at the service of God must begin by resolving the question of these three temptations.

You will say that the Creator has given us a physical body, a heart and a mind, and that we must provide them with the nourishment they need. Yes, of course, this is indispensable. But there are different kinds of nourishment and different ways of procuring it. It is precisely here that we need faith, hope and love to guide us in our choice of food and of the means to obtain it, for hope relates to the physical body, faith to the astral body, and love to the intellect or mental body.

Bread, in the broadest sense of the word, is thus the symbol of whatever enables us to maintain our existence on the physical plane. And what is the fate of those who do not put their hope in God? They are fearful for their physical security and have only one idea in mind: to look after their business, pile up reserve stocks, increase their profits. Not only do they allow themselves to be completely absorbed by the most prosaic cares, but they are led to be unjust and dishonest toward others. They have no scruples about short-changing others or riding roughshod over them, and in this way they close themselves to any spiritual nourishment.

To hope in God is to free oneself from all fear for tomorrow: "Will we have what we need to eat, to clothe ourselves and to have a roof over our heads?" In the Sermon on the Mount Jesus warns us against this fear for the morrow: *So do not worry about tomorrow, for tomorrow*

*will bring worries of its own. Today's trouble is
enough for today.*[4]

If hope is related to the physical body, faith,
for its part, is linked to the heart. And the heart
is the temple in which God abides. When Jesus
answered, *Do not put the Lord your God to the
test*, it was a declaration of faith in the God that
dwelt within him, and he refused to put him to
the test. Faith does not consist in throwing
yourself into the abyss in the conviction that
God will send angels to cushion your fall.
Anyone who imagines that God protects fools
who deliberately expose themselves to danger is
simply entertaining false beliefs. And the reason
why human beings suffer so many disap-
pointments in their lives, why they so often meet
with failure instead of the success they counted
on, is that they confuse faith and belief.

Finally, the third temptation, which is related
to the head, can only be overcome by love. The
devil had taken Jesus to the top of a high
mountain. In us, it is our head which represents
the mountain. Those who reach the summit
possess knowledge, authority and power. But
history has demonstrated that those who obtain
power have great difficulty in resisting all the
possibilities which open up before them –
money, pleasure and glory – and think that they

4 Mt. 6, 34.

now have the right to do whatever they please. So many truly outstanding people have succumbed in the end, vanquished by their own pride. Only the love of the Being of all beings can shield us from these dangers. It is he who has given us all our faculties and talents, and if we love him sincerely and deeply, that love will preserve us from pride.

Hope, faith and love are therefore the only forces that make it possible for us to go through life in the best physical, psychic and spiritual conditions. Hope in God preserves us from the anxieties of our material existence. Faith in him frees us from the grip of illusions. Finally, love of him enables us to reach and secure our hold on the summit without risk of falling.

Study the lives of those who have faith, hope and love, and see how they work, how they grow in beauty and vitality, how they manage to face up to difficulties and overcome trials, finding in each occasion a new opportunity for enrichment. These three virtues seem very remote to you, because your understanding of them is too abstract. You fail to sense that they constitute the three pillars of your psychic life. To help you to understand and sense their full importance, I will give you an exercise to do.

Faith, hope and love are called "theological" virtues because it is through them that we can be in touch with God. Here again the trouble is that human beings have a tendency to see God as an abstraction. Most people – if they do not actually picture him as an old man with a white beard who spends his time recording their good and especially their bad deeds, in order to reward or punish them – do not know quite how to envisage him. But I have never ceased to tell you: the best possible depiction of God is the sun, the one that pours forth life, light and warmth. Only the life, light and warmth of the sun can give us some idea of the power, wisdom and love of God. And it is up to us to establish a relationship with that divine power, wisdom and light. How can we do this? Through hope, faith and love. Yes, it is through our hope, our faith and our love that we make contact with the quintessence of the Godhead: Wisdom, Power and Love.

Here then is the exercise: Recite the following prayer slowly, concentrating on every word: "Dear God, I love your wisdom; I have faith in your love; I hope in your power." Our love puts us in touch with divine wisdom; through faith we communicate with divine love, and through hope we are in contact with divine power. These notions are very simple, but they need further explanation.

"Lord, I love your wisdom." Wisdom has an affinity with the cold, and love with warmth. Our heart needs a great deal of warmth, a great deal of fervor and enthusiasm, but it senses that it is ignorant, that it lacks discernment and restraint, and that it is apt to make a great many mistakes for which it suffers. So it must love and seek to acquire what it lacks and needs: wisdom.

"I believe in your love." We do not need to love love, but we do need to believe in it. A child believes in its mother's love; this is why it feels safe with her. Love and faith are linked. If you believe in someone he will love you; if you love someone he will believe in you. And because the love of the Creator is the very foundation of the universe, it is in him and in him alone that we can have absolute faith. Our faith in beings and things can repose on a firm foundation only if we have placed our trust first of all in divine love.

"I hope in your power." How often people say that it is hope that keeps them alive! At the beginning of every year, people exchange good wishes and express the hope that the new year will be better than the one before and bring solutions to all their problems. But what are these hopes based on? Money... arms... weak, unstable people! This is why they are always disappointed. The fact is that we can count only on the true strength, the true stability of divine omnipotence.

And now, look at the way this prayer

establishes links with the divine world. When you say, "Lord, I love your wisdom", you link your love to divine wisdom and God allows you to be wiser because of that love. When you say, "Lord, I believe in your love", your faith attracts divine love and God loves you because you believe in him. When you say, "I hope in your power", your hope appeals to God's power, and it begins to protect you because of that hope.

Hope, faith and love correspond respectively to the form, the content and the meaning. Hope is linked to form (the physical body), faith to the content (the heart), and love to the meaning (the intellect). It is the form which prepares and preserves the content. The content brings strength, and the only *raison d'être* of strength is that it has meaning.

When human beings are disappointed by events and dissatisfied with their lot, they tend to project their hopes into the future: "Soon... in a few days... in a few months... things will get better." There is no doubt that hope is the very last thing to be abandoned, but while we hang on, waiting for things to get better, we need to count on something reliable. In order to hang on we need not only to believe, but also to quicken the life within us, to find warmth and enthusiasm, and it is love that gives us this. If it does not, our hope can be no more than a flight from reality, and one day it, too, will abandon us.

If we want never to lose hope, we must keep faith and love alive within us and call on them for help when difficulties arise. But human beings usually do just the opposite: at the least little disappointment, the slightest set-back, they close their hearts and lose faith, and all hope abandons them... except, of course, the hope of avenging themselves, by means that are not always highly commendable! That does not worry them; they find all kinds of arguments to justify their hostile, vindictive attitude. How can they be brought to understand that, on the contrary, they will overcome their difficulties only with faith, hope and love? Yes, difficulties are sent to us precisely for this: to develop these three virtues, on the condition that God is the object of that faith, hope and love. These three virtues can be compared to the three facets of a crystal prism, and the divine presence is like the ray of sunlight that falls on this prism and is diffracted into the seven colours.

In one of his talks, *The Seven Great Forces*, Peter Deunov said: "Human beings are very easily discouraged, and to justify this discouragement they blame circumstances. No, the underlying cause of their discouragement does not lie in external conditions; it lies in the fact that they have too little hope, too little faith and too little love. To tread the path of life steadfastly they need to strengthen within themselves the three sources of faith, hope and love. Where are these sources to be found? In the brain. Yes, we have three centers in our brains which are the conductors of faith, hope and love, for faith, hope and love are cosmic forces."

The brain is the site of all our faculties and all our virtues, and because faith, hope and love link us directly to God, they are located in the upper part of the head. Love is in the center of the crown; slightly forward and on each side is the center of faith, and slightly to the rear and on each side is the center of hope.

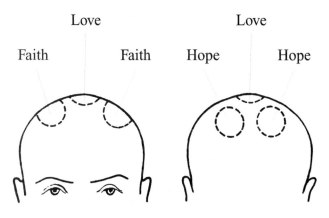

The Master Peter Deunov also said: "Man must wear these three inner garments: hope, which is the human garment; faith, which is the angelic garment, and love, which is the divine garment. I call holy any one who wears these three garments of faith, hope and love." And on another occasion, he said: "Hope answers the question of a day; faith answers the question of centuries, and love is the force that embraces eternity." Why did the Master say that hope answers the question of a day? This relates to the Gospel passage I quoted earlier, in which Jesus said: *Do not worry about tomorrow, for tomorrow will bring worries of its own. Today's trouble is enough for today.* As you see, everything is connected.

Faith, hope and love... How many of our contemporaries have recourse to these virtues to resolve the problems of their everyday lives? They rely on the progress of science and technology, on the law courts, and so on. But faith, hope and love? Never! That was good enough for the Middle Ages... but these are modern men and women. Well, I have no objection, but they will see... In the long run they will see whether science, technology, insurance policies and the courts can solve their problems for them and give them happiness. I am not saying that we should return to the past and reject all innovations. If the universal spirit that controls the evolution of creatures has allowed mankind to develop in this way, it is for a reason. It is because it considers this experience necessary; humanity has to be exposed to this. Once it has completed the experience, it will turn back to the Creator, wiser and enriched by all its new acquisitions. Human beings, created "in the image of God", must develop in all their dimensions in order, one day, to resemble God. And before they can resemble God, their faith, hope and love must be put to the test of matter with all its snares and seductions.

Those who live according to faith, hope and love are living in conformity with universal laws. It is by faith, hope and love that you construct your existence. Appeal to these cosmic forces and ask for their help, adopt them as your counselors, for in that way you will become really useful to yourselves and to the whole world.

2

THE MUSTARD SEED

Sometimes, when someone throws himself into an enterprise with conviction, enthusiasm and tenacity, we say that he has a "faith that moves mountains". Those who say this have perhaps forgotten – and some have never known – that this expression comes from the Gospels. One day, Jesus reproached his disciples for their disbelief, saying: *I tell you, if you have faith the size of a mustard seed, you will say to this mountain, "Move from here to there," and it will move; and nothing will be impossible for you.*[1] But how should these words be interpreted?

Once upon a time there was an old peasant woman who was very irritated by a small hill which blocked the view from her house. Every morning, when she opened the shutters, she could not help cursing that hill. Now that she was old and rather crippled, she could no longer

1 Mt. 17, 20.

go and keep an eye on her cows grazing in the meadow; if that rotten hill were not there, she could at least have seen them from her window. Then, one Sunday morning at Mass, the priest gave a long sermon about this verse from the Gospel: *If you have faith the size of a mustard seed, you will say to this mountain...* The old woman was delighted. At last, she thought, she had found the solution. That evening, before closing her shutters, she said a short prayer and then spoke severely to the hill: "Tomorrow, when I get up, I don't want to see you there any more. Is that understood?" After which she went calmly to bed. As soon as she awoke the next day, she hurried to open her shutters... The hill had not moved. But then, once she had given vent to her disappointment, she muttered, "Oh, it doesn't surprise me. I thought as much!"

Of course, the old lady was right to doubt, for no one has ever been able to move a mountain, and Jesus never wanted us to move mountains around. We have to take the image figuratively. The proof that it is figurative is the fact that Jesus himself never moved any mountains. No one has the right to do that – in any case what possible reason could there be to do so? And what would happen if we had to judge the faith of human beings according to their power to move mountains? What upheavals in the landscape and the climate!

Rivers and lakes would also change places, with all the consequences that this would entail... No, we must leave the mountains alone: they have a role to play where they are.

You will wonder, "But then, why did Jesus say that?" In fact, there is even another place in the Gospels where Jesus says to his disciples: *Truly I tell you, if you have faith and do not doubt... if you say to this mountain, 'Be lifted up and thrown into the sea,' it will be done.*[2]

How can we understand if he did not explain? You must remember that at the end of his Gospel, St John reveals that if one were to report in detail everything that Jesus said and did, the world itself could not contain all the books that would be written. Even if this is exaggerated, it shows that the Gospels are far from being complete; they give no more than the skeleton of Jesus' teaching, and it is up to us to clothe that skeleton in flesh, in the light of initiatic science.

So, since Jesus did not have physical mountains in mind, what mountains was he talking about? Our inner, psychic mountains. All the obstacles and difficulties that we have allowed to pile up within us – these are the mountains that bar the way ahead and prevent us from making progress. Perhaps you will say,

2 Mt. 21, 21.

"All right, now we understand: this image of the mountain refers to the psychic plane. But does faith – even very strong faith – have the ability to move a mountain of difficulties and problems that have accumulated in the course of many incarnations?" Well who said anything about moving them in one fell swoop? If you could interpret the image of the mustard seed, you would realize that that is not what Jesus was saying.

So let us look at another passage in the Gospels, in which Jesus talks about the mustard seed:

The kingdom of heaven is like a mustard seed that someone took and sowed in his field; it is the smallest of all the seeds, but when it has grown it is the greatest of shrubs and becomes a tree, so that the birds of the air come and make nests in its branches.[3]

Yes, the mustard seed is tiny, but what do we do with a seed? We plant it, and once it is in the ground, it sprouts and grows. In Jesus' image of the mustard seed, the important point us that it is a seed, and that the destiny of a seed is to be sown. Once planted, it is not inactive; if it is healthy and robust, it sprouts and becomes a tree. But not all at once... it takes time.

Because a mountain is huge and a mustard

3 Mt. 13, 31-32.

seed minute, those who read this parable are so struck by the enormous discrepancy in size of the two that they often stop there, and this is why they cannot interpret the parable correctly. In order to interpret it correctly we have to begin by reflecting on the nature and properties of a seed. If someone whose faith is no bigger than a mustard seed is going to be capable one day of moving mountains, it is because once that seed is sown in his heart and soul it grows and expands. When it becomes a tree, all the birds of heaven – that is, all the luminous entities of the invisible world – come and dwell in it. And these entities do not come empty-handed. They bring with them all heavenly gifts – wisdom, love, purity, peace, strength – and it is thanks to those gifts that the person gradually becomes capable of moving mountains.

It is essential for a Christian to understand what Jesus meant when he spoke of a faith capable of moving mountains. Without this understanding one can only repeat words that have been emptied of all meaning. Just as Jesus' words in the Sermon on the Mount have been emptied of meaning: *Be perfect, therefore, as your heavenly Father is perfect.*[4] Human beings are so weak and irresolute, how could they possibly move mountains? And they have so

4 Mt. 5, 48.

many weaknesses and faults, how could they ever attain the perfection of the heavenly Father? It is just not possible! And so, because of a lack of understanding, because of negligence and laziness – yes, especially because of laziness – people disregard the quintessence of Christ's teaching. It is so much easier to emphasize human weaknesses and imperfections, deluding ourselves that in doing so we are demonstrating lucidity, commonsense... so-called modesty. But Jesus had none of that modesty in regard to human beings created in the image of God – he had the most exalted ambitions for them. If they have the will, if they make the necessary efforts, they will one day attain the perfection of the heavenly Father. And if they have faith, they will one day move mountains. In other words, all powers will be given to them, but the first of these will be the power over themselves.

Faith, therefore, is like a seed which we have to sow, but it is not just any seed. It is not so easy to recognize the seed that will become a tree in which the birds of the air will take shelter. On the contrary, it is very difficult to distinguish it from the seeds of all kinds of beliefs and superstitions. This is why Christians have not yet moved many mountains. The first thing we have to do, therefore, is learn to recognize the seed of faith.

3

FAITH AND BELIEF

One day, a parish priest was talking to his parishioners, most of whom were very wealthy. He told them: "Dear brethren, as you can see, our church is old and needs many repairs. But it is going to cost a lot of money, so I want you to think about it and see what we can do..." With one accord, his parishioners replied that they would ask God to help them find the necessary money. "What!" exclaimed the priest indignantly; "You are billionaires and you want to bother God to find a sum of money that you can very easily find for yourselves?"

Well, this is what many believers call faith: to ask for divine intervention in solving their problems when they could perfectly well do so themselves if only they would decide to make the necessary efforts. Although many altruistic people may pray for peace in the world, for people to be less unhappy, they rely principally on God to assure their own well-being, comfort and security.

When people are leaving for a vacation, for instance, they close the door of their house and say a brief prayer: "Lord, please guard my house..." And then, on their return, they are furious when they find that they have had "visitors". "How come God did not keep watch?" Oh yes, we think the Deity should be a janitor. He should have kept an eye on the house while the owners were gallivanting elsewhere.

You will say, "But is prayer not an expression of faith? Should we not pray?" Yes, you should pray. But prayer does not consist in making demands on God. He has given us all the means necessary, both material and spiritual, to look after our own needs and even those of others, and prayer should serve simply to help us to rise to where those means are to be found. One might say that God has already done his part a long time ago. It is not his "job" to give us what we need; it is up to us to look for it. What is the point of asking him for health or the affection of others if we continue to live in a way that makes us ill or disagreeable? And what is the good of praying for peace if we continue to carry a veritable battle-field within us wherever we go? True, prayer is an expression of faith, but faith must be understood as the force that incites human beings to surpass, to transcend themselves. It seems that there is one kind of faith that is inspired by effort and activity, and another that is inspired by laziness. Many people call faith something that, in reality, is no more than a belief, sometimes even an aberration.

Seeking to excuse their blunders, mistakes and failures, people will tell you: "But I believed this or that..." Ah yes, believe, believe... but their believing has only served to lead them astray. And what is worse, these "believers" will continue to believe, and will continue to be led astray. Until when? Until they learn to replace their beliefs by faith, true faith, the faith that is founded on knowledge. It is clear that we instinctively understand the difference between belief and faith, for we often say, "I believe such and such", when in fact we are expressing a doubt. If we say, "I believe he is coming tomorrow," it means that, in fact, we are not sure: it is a belief. And the question, "Do you believe that ...?" shows that you are exploring unknown territory. Faith, true faith functions in a domain that is known, in which one has long-standing experience thanks to patient efforts.

Take a very simple example. A gardener has various seeds. He sows them and knows without risk of error that he will harvest lettuces, radishes and so on. His predictions come true because his knowledge is based on study and experience. But many people who believe are like gardeners who expect to harvest something they have never sown, or who sow carrot seeds expecting them to produce leeks. They expect something impossible because they have neither knowledge nor experience. One can harvest only what one has sown. Only then can one have faith. As you see, here again we come back to the image of the mustard seed used by Jesus in the parable.

So, we must not delude ourselves. If we meet with failure instead of the success we had expected, it means either that we did not sow any seeds, or that we sowed the wrong kind. This is true in every domain, even that of religion. Many people call themselves believers, but when one sees the contradictions they are struggling with, one wonders what exactly they understand by that. How can we help them? If only they could bring themselves to admit that they are mistaken, that they still do not know what true faith is, it would already be a step in the right direction. Instead, they wax indignant and tell you that they belong to such and such a religion and believe this or that. They will give you a list of all the prayers they say, the services they attend, and so on... How can you cast doubts on their faith? Unhappy people, always ill, gossiping, jealous and bitter, who poison their own lives and the lives of those around them... but they have faith!

Well, people who are so unenlightened do not know that faith and success go together, and by "success" I mean the victory over one's inner difficulties and obstacles. They have never heard – or perhaps they have forgotten – Jesus' parable of the mustard seed, and not only have they never moved mountains but they are buried beneath them. That which they call faith is in fact no more than beliefs or personal convictions. But their personal convictions often have as little foundation as their beliefs. Convictions of course are a force because of the energy they release. People who are convinced emit waves that carry off everything in their path, just as a strong wind sweeps away dead leaves. This is why people often allow themselves to be led by a madman. He manages to impose his convictions on them, because, as they say, "he is absolutely certain." But they never ask where this may lead them...

So we must not confuse faith and belief. Unfortunately, most people who think they have faith do in fact confuse the two. It is quite possible to hold beliefs, even religious beliefs, without actually having faith. To have faith is to know which seeds to choose and then to sow them within oneself so that they become magnificent trees and produce delicious fruit. If you have no harvest – or if you harvest nothing but thorns and thistles – it is because you are not yet a good "sower", not yet one who has true faith.

To distinguish between faith and belief one needs certain criteria. The first criterion of faith is that it makes people better, more stable, more harmonious and more concerned for others. Also, it must be a process that is continually developing, like the tree in the parable, so that the birds of the air – that is, virtues and luminous entities – come and nest in its branches.

Heaven does not require that people be perfect, only that they work to perfect themselves. One day everyone should be able to say, "Now I understand. I am sowing these seeds in my soul – luminous thoughts and feelings, the love of a high ideal – and I shall continue to watch over them, to water them, warm them, and nourish them with all that is best in me. I know that the universe is governed by laws, and that one of these laws says that in the long run every seed produces fruit." That is an expression of true faith. And it means that, whatever religion you may belong to – Christianity, Islam, Judaism, Hinduism, or any other – as long as you have not yet understood this law and are not applying it in your life, you possess not faith but only beliefs which cannot get you very far. Or rather, they can take you a long way, but down the road of laziness, failure, rebellion and so on.

Belief is ineffectual because it is something that comes from the outside, from the periphery of our being, and sooner or later it crumbles in the face of reality. Faith, on the other hand, comes from within, from the core of our being, and it is from there that it derives its efficacy. What a mistake, therefore, to imagine that faith is only good for people who are ignorant, naïve or slightly retarded, to think that to abandon such so-called irrational beliefs is a step forward in the evolution of humanity. On the contrary, faith is founded on knowledge of the laws, and what higher science is there than knowledge of the laws?

To have faith is to build one's life on a firm foundation, because one knows the laws. Those who have faith sense that they are treading a clearly-defined path. They choose to follow this path because they have learned the truth of the law of cause and effect. And while they are busy building something strong and beautiful, they have no time for the stupid things people say or do all around them. All their attention is concentrated on the work they have undertaken, so that when difficulties arise, the results already obtained through that work give them the strength to overcome them.

So many people are troubled. They are sure of nothing. They see danger everywhere because they feel they have been thrown into existence as though into a complex system whose rules they cannot fathom. This is simply because they have not learned to work with the laws, and are thus unable to clear the obstacles from their path and safeguard their future. It is impossible to build a good future if the present is bad, for there is no separation between the two. Indeed, as long as one has not learned to build the present on a firm foundation, there is every reason to fear the future.

How can you not be afraid when you do not know where you are going, when you have no certainty about anything, when you are completely in the dark? Darkness is the source of all fear, for in darkness everything appears as a threat.

The life of a human being can be compared to trekking through a dense forest or climbing a tall mountain. There are such great efforts to be made, so many dangers to be confronted before reaching the goal. And if we have to go through the forest or climb the mountain in the dark, we are in danger of losing our way, of being attacked by wild animals, of falling into an ambush, of tumbling down a precipice, and so on. In the dark the dangers are real, but the greatest danger is the fear that originates within us because we do not know how to interpret the sounds and vague shapes we sense around us. We can be sure of nothing, so we live in a state of apprehension and anxiety, convincing ourselves at every moment that something dreadful is about to happen.

And just as belief opens a door within us, fear gives power to that which we fear, fear gives it the conditions it needs to harm us. Well, there you have an image of the existence of those who do not possess the light of faith, of true faith, which, in reality, is a knowledge that brings security and peace. Even though we have to contend with trials, if we know how things work we can go forward in peace, full of hope for the future.

And this brings us to the relationship between faith and hope, that is, between present and future. Here again is a new light on Jesus' words: *Do not worry about tomorrow, for tomorrow will bring worries of its own. Today's trouble is enough for today.*[1] Do your duty today, knowing that it is the best thing to do, and that it is enough. You have no need to worry about tomorrow, for tomorrow is necessarily linked to the day that went before, so it too will be ordered and harmonious. Here again, it is as though you sowed a seed, and that seed will bear fruit.

How wrong people are to assert that the criteria of faith cannot be known! They only need to observe themselves and what goes on in their psychic life as well as in their physical and social life. Whenever they find themselves in a blind alley, it means that they did not know where to place their faith. Is it really so difficult to understand that a cause always produces consequences of the same nature, and that if we want to know why certain events occur or why things happen to us, we should always look for the causes? This is the criterion of faith. Without this we have to be content to flounder in beliefs. Yes, we believe that just because we have put oil in the frying pan and the pan on the stove, the fish will suddenly jump into it, even though it is still in the

1 Mt. 6, 34.

sea. No, it is time to get rid of these illusory beliefs, for they are inevitably followed by disillusionment. Beliefs are the product of personal wishes or of tricks of the mind, and they lead inevitably to doubt, anxiety and distrust. Faith, by contrast, is an absolute certainty which always leads to positive results.

True faith, therefore, is based on knowledge gained from experience. By nature, however, human beings are more drawn to belief than to knowledge, for belief is spontaneous and instinctive, whereas knowledge requires study, reflection and experience. Thus belief always precedes knowledge. As soon as one knows something one has gone a step beyond belief, and one's belief will then be applied to something further away, until there too, knowledge catches up and replaces it. Knowledge is like the horizon: the nearer we get to it, the farther it recedes... but this is how we make progress.

At first sight, you will find it difficult to distinguish clearly between belief and faith, for the line that separates them is poorly defined. They merge into each other, just as the physical gradually merges into the psychic without it being possible to see just where one begins and the other ends. The line between them is no clearer than that which divides the colours of the spectrum. Red, for instance, is not orange, but it is impossible to put one's finger exactly on the dividing line.

Similarly, although faith is not the same as belief, it remains very closely linked to it.

We do need a certain number of beliefs in our existence. They are a support-system for our emotional and intellectual life. Without these props our life would be impossible; it would be like trying to walk through quicksands. Both inwardly and outwardly we need to believe that there is firm ground under our feet. This is why, even though some of our beliefs may be illusory, it is always useful to believe good things. It helps us to maintain a constructive attitude. What really matters is to become more conscious, to replace vague beliefs by veritable knowledge, and not to be as naïve at forty as we were at twenty.

We might even say, therefore, that faith is a work that has to be done on one's beliefs, and that those who fail to undertake this work often become the prey of superstitions, for beliefs and superstitions go together. Since human beings always need to believe in something, those who do not understand what faith really is cling to all kinds of little things: they adopt an object as a good luck charm, think that a certain number or day of the week is favorable or unfavorable, interpret an encounter with this or that person as a sign of good or bad luck, and so on. I do not deny that one can attribute a certain significance to objects, numbers, days or encounters, but these things can never take the place of a faith based on

the great laws that govern our psychic and
spiritual life.

Shall I define superstition for you? To be
superstitious is to think that you can harvest
something that you have not sown. To have
genuine faith, on the other hand, is to wait,
knowing that one will harvest what one has sown,
whether in this life or in another, or even through
one's children. If you sow good seed in fertile soil
in the right season, it will sprout and grow. Some
seeds will, perhaps, be lost, but the majority will
grow and bear fruit. So many men and women
who have never done any intellectual, emotional
or physical work hope to reap a rich harvest, and
when they realize their failure they cry out against
the injustice of it. But whose fault is it? Those who
sow and plant are never disappointed. If some are
disappointed it is because their expectations were
unrealistic

And since to have faith is to cultivate seeds,
the day will come when those seeds will nourish
you, whereas in the long run beliefs will leave you
hungry. Belief is like hypnosis. If you hypnotize
someone you can persuade him, for example, that
he is having a good meal. When he comes round
from the trance he will be able to tell you exactly
what was on the menu and how good it was, and
yet his stomach is empty, and if he were to go on
like that he would soon collapse. Well, beliefs
deceive people in exactly the same way, whereas

faith gives them real fruit to eat every day – nourishing fruit that is the result of the work they have done.

Those who are content with beliefs will always be inwardly emaciated, under-developed and shaky, however physically vigorous they may be. Beliefs are not nourishing. Only faith is nourishing, and in order to obtain it we have to study, experiment and exert ourselves. If in ancient times initiation was given only to certain people, it was not so much that it involved revealing secrets to them that could not be entrusted to others, but rather because they possessed certain qualities which enabled them to achieve something with those revelations. Spiritual truths enrich only those whose intellect is capable of understanding them, whose hearts yearn for them, above all, who have the will to begin this work and to persevere in it. To others they are of no benefit... they can even be harmful.

If people reduce religion to a few articles of faith without reference to the experience and actions which should accompany them, they are separating religion from faith, and are left with nothing but beliefs... which can never save anyone. The lazy will never be saved. With no work, no effort, no experimentation, what results can you expect? As long as believers do no more than repeat their formulas, gestures and unintelligible rites, their faith will never move mountains, never work any miracles. And when I speak of miracles, I am not speaking of raising the dead but of transforming oneself, of raising oneself to life.

It is time you learned not to confuse the reality of faith with the illusion of beliefs. If your health improves, if your mind becomes clearer, if you become stronger and your love grows, it means that you are nourished by faith. As for the beliefs that you imagine to be nourishment, they are like the cotton candy sold at fairs... children love it, but not only does it not nourish them, it also spoils their teeth. That is how many people absorb beliefs. They swallow tons of dreams and promises which contain nothing solid; they are all fluff and sugar. They believe, they believe, they never stop believing – and the results they obtain are in direct contradiction to what they believe.

Believe? No, you must not believe any more; you must know. Faith is a condensation of a knowledge that is perennial. If you have no knowledge, you have no faith. So study, become stronger, work every day with the divine virtues – love, wisdom, truth, kindness and justice – for these are the seeds you must sow as you go along. And at the end of the road, resurrection, the fullness of life, will be waiting for you.

4

SCIENCE AND RELIGION

For centuries, a ceaseless battle raged in the West between science and religion. For a long time, religion triumphed because it was the stronger. It was religion that laid down the law – to the point where any new discovery was condemned on the pretext that it was in contradiction with the Bible or with Church dogma. The few intrepid beings who dared to doubt, for example, that God created the world in six days, or who claimed that the earth revolved round the sun, risked being burned at the stake. And then, little by little, the situation was reversed, As science gradually advanced, it gained the upper hand and retaliated by pouring scorn on religion and forcing it to beat a retreat. It is common knowledge today that religion has lost much of its influence. Some, of course, regret this while others rejoice. But neither regrets nor satisfaction is going to answer the questions that torment human beings.

To simplify things, let's say that science concerns the visible world and religion the invisible world. The lack of understanding that prevails between men of science and men of faith comes from the fact that the former base their convictions on visible, objective reality, whereas the latter base theirs on an invisible, subjective reality. But both points of view are incomplete, because each has a tendency to give priority to one aspect and play down the other.

The universe is an entity which human beings can grasp from the outside by means of science, and from the inside by means of religion, because they themselves are entities capable of living both in the objective and the subjective worlds. Instead of opposing each other, science and religion should complete each other. In any case, it is not science that opposes religion or *vice versa*, it is scientists and men of religion who oppose each other, because both camps possess incomplete knowledge.

Science will never wipe out religion any more than religion was able to wipe out science, for they are founded on identical laws. There can be neither division nor contradiction between the two. Divisions and contradictions exist only in the minds of ignorant people who do not know how God created the universe. Science properly understood can only help believers to concentrate on the essentials, and religion properly understood gives its true dimension to science. Each has its specific function, and they should support each other rather than rejecting and trying to destroy each other. In any case, they will never succeed in doing so. The battles between them are sterile and a waste of time. Henceforth each human being should be inwardly both scientific and religious. For if science and religion are to cease waging war in society, they must first call a truce in each human being. It is here that the ravages are greatest. When a man of faith opposes a man of science – and vice versa – he believes he is attacking an adversary exterior to himself. No, not at all! He is attacking himself.

Unbelievers have a false understanding of religion. And in fact, the understanding of most believers is equally inexact, for they restrict it, for the most part, to a set of dogmas and rites. In reality, religion is first and foremost a science based on the nature of human beings created in the image of God. This is why it would be true to say that the foundations of religion are an integral part of a human being. When God created us, he put his seal on us, and we can do nothing to get rid of it; it is written into our basic structure. In this sense, human beings are not absolutely free; they cannot escape from this imprint, from this basic design on which they are built. On the other hand, they have the greatest possible freedom to manifest the divine predestination they bear within them. This is why there are so many religions which, depending on where and when they came into being, have taken on such a rich diversity of forms.

A scientist would say that only those things that can be observed, calculated, measured, weighed, compared and classified are real and worthy of attention. All the rest is of dubious interest and should be ignored. Very well, but this puts an enormous restriction on the scope of his consciousness, for two-thirds (for the sake of argument, let's say two-thirds) of the life of a human being is taken up by activities which cannot be weighed or measured. Yes, two-thirds of our time is spent in living: nothing more. And if that two-thirds of life merits no attention, is of no interest, one wonders how a scientist can go on living. He breathes, eats, drinks, sleeps and walks; he has thoughts, feelings, sensations and desires; he meets other people, talks to them – sometimes embraces them – and he does all of that without wondering whether he is doing it scientifically. How can he bear to live a life so much of which is not scientific? He should refuse!

By putting such a high price on a scientific view of the world in which priority is given to the study of nature, of the physical world, a world which is outside them – or, at least, which is no more than the physical envelope of their deepest self – human beings disperse themselves on the outskirts of their being. They do not realize that they are losing their center, that essential core of their being which not only holds them in equilibrium, but which links them to the Source of universal life. Of course, there is no law against seeing the universe as a vast field of investigation and experiment provided for them by the Creator. But it is not by throwing themselves body and soul into the study of physics, chemistry, biology, zoology, astronomy, etc., that they will acquire a taste for divine life. While they are so busy satisfying their curiosity, time passes, their life moves on and their strength diminishes.

However great the possibilities available to scientists to explore and exploit matter, an initial period of awe and wonder brought about by their discoveries will always be followed by a sense of inner emptiness. For none of what can be touched, embraced or understood by the intellect has the power to fulfil us. Only immensity, mystery, only that which is invisible and intangible, only the unknown can satisfy and fulfil the human soul. This is where true science lies.

True science is not the product of intellectual acquisitions, it is a direct knowledge of human

nature, of the psychic and spiritual structure of
human beings, of their subtle bodies, their
highest aspirations and their links with the whole
of the universe. There is no reason to reject some
phenomena on the pretext that they cannot be
classified as lending themselves to observation
and calculation. The spiritual life is said to be a
non-scientific phenomenon. All right. If you
want to be permanently dissatisfied and in a
vacuum, pay attention only to what is considered
"scientific".

As science advanced, people began to think
that it could explain and find solutions for all of
mankind's problems. It is true that it has brought
tremendous improvements in many areas, but it
cannot be said to have produced any fundamental improvement in the human condition,
because it concerns only the physical – and to a
limited extent the psychic – world. It does not
affect the soul or spirit... and that is as it should
be, as these are not its province. In a very short
time, thanks to some extremely sophisticated
instruments, science has made astonishing
discoveries both in matters infinitely great and
infinitesimally small, and these discoveries have
deluded some people into thinking that science
could well take the place of religion. But
although astronauts now explore cosmic reaches
that for thousands of years human beings
thought of as the abode of God; although

physicists can now pierce the innermost secrets of matter; although biologists achieve greater and greater power over life... none of this entitles human beings to believe themselves the equal of God or to declare that he does not exist – or that he is dead – and that creation is the result of chance.

I put all the philosophers and scientists who think that the universe and man came about by chance in the same basket as Christians who expect to harvest when they have never sown. The error is the same in both cases. In one it is a question of consequences without a cause; in the other, of creation without an author. There is no call for self-styled intelligentsia and scientists to scoff at the naiveté of believers: their own convictions are just as ridiculous.

Whatever the advances of science, it will never be able to replace or destroy religion, any more than religion was able to prevent the progress of science. There is a link between the two attitudes, and each must help to enrich and enlighten the other. Those who attempt to separate them or set them up against each other are making a great mistake. God has not put into the universe he created – or into man made in his own image – two incompatible realities. But we cannot really understand unless we adjust a certain number of inner attitudes.

One often hears public figures expressing

indignation at the fact that in the 20th Century human beings have still not managed to rid themselves of beliefs which they deem to be irrational. In fact, one cannot deny that after a period of materialism and scientism, more and more people are turning back to religion, spirituality and mysticism, and that this tendency sometimes assumes very confused and irrational forms. Even religious authorities are worried about it. They sense their helplessness in the face of these new trends over which they have no control. Well, the responsibility for this situation belongs both to the religious authorities themselves, who have been more concerned with extending the ascendancy of their church than of responding to the real needs of souls and spirits, and to the scientists and their materialistic philosophies. It is time they ceased to lament a situation that they have both helped to create and joined forces to find a solution.

Human beings can be fulfilled only by immensity, infinity. Although they may find that some things which are visible, fixed, measured and classified are useful and interesting, even indispensable, in the long run they realize that they can satisfy only part of their being; they can never be enough to fill a whole existence. Why are children so fond of fairy-tales? And why do most adults seek refuge whenever possible in strange, fantastic, irrational worlds? Because this corresponds to an innate human need. Human beings have been created to live in the two worlds, objective and subjective, material and spiritual, visible and invisible, and consequently not only do they possess the ability to communicate with both worlds, but they need them both. However, one must not confuse the two: the reality we perceive by the five senses is not the same as that which we perceive by means of our spiritual senses. These are two different worlds, and we need two different types of instrument to perceive them.

Scientists must be content to study, observe and report the results of their observations. That is all. They have no business making declarations about the psychic, moral or spiritual life of man. There is a borderline that they may not cross. With the means at their disposal they are not entitled to replace religion by science, still less to destroy it. What they may destroy – and it would be a good thing if they did – are false beliefs. True religion has no need to burden itself with error and superstition, and true science can do no harm to true religion. God will not be insulted if you do not believe that he created the world in six days... far from it, in fact, since he never ceases creating it.

In any case, to attempt to combat religion in the name of objectivity and reason is a lost cause. It is no more possible to do away with religious sentiment than with any other human sentiment. Here again is a realm in which reason is not the only consideration, because, as I have said, a sense of the sacred, the need to feel connected to the divine world from which we came is an integral part of every human being. You can try to deny this, to tear it out by the roots, but although the attempt may seem to succeed, success will be only momentary. It will not last; and the only thing you can do then will be to take stock of the damage that has been inflicted not only on individuals but on society as a whole.

But there is something more: have all these people who advocate objectivity and reason succeeded in establishing them in their own lives? Look at them: they are struggling in the midst of anxiety, fear, rage, jealousy and every kind of uncontrolled passion. Where are objectivity and reason in all that? And yet they accept these inferior sentiments; they even seem to find them quite natural. Whereas the noble sentiments inspired by faith in a supreme Entity who created heaven and earth, trust, gratitude, love and adoration for that Being are in their view ridiculous. Like the intellect, reason can be very useful in helping to introduce order into the realm of feelings. You might say that it is needed to tidy things up... Yes, to tidy things up, not to throw them away. When you tidy your house, you move furniture and other objects in order to vacuum or dust, but then you put them back where they belong; you don't throw them out of the window. And for yourselves too, if you call on reason to tidy your interior, it is not in order to get rid of a genuine religious sentiment, but, on the contrary, to see it more clearly in all its glory, once you have done away with your false beliefs.

Materialistic theories may seduce people for a moment and even sever their ties with immensity, but only temporarily. Whether all these "great minds" like it or not, the Creator has designed human beings in such a way that they cannot do without him. If they think they can, it will be for only a brief moment. They will soon sense that they have mutilated themselves and will be obliged to turn back to another conception of the world and of themselves. It is pointless, therefore, to waste time raging against incorrigible people who need to believe in a Creator of the universe, in invisible worlds peopled by spiritual entities, in life after death, in the power of prayer... they will remain incorrigible. Yes, because they are in touch with the reality of man and of the universe, and no one can do away with that reality.

What do we know about human beings? It

has taken thousands of years to get to know their physical bodies, and even now we cannot be sure that everything has been discovered. As for their psychic and spiritual bodies, practically nothing is known, except by initiates and mystics. You will say, "But psychologists, psychiatrists, psychoanalysts... they know a great deal about the human psyche." Well, without wishing to cast doubt on their learning, I would like to point out that their profession deals with those who are ill. That is fine, but I look at the question from a different point of view: would it not be better to give human beings knowledge that would enable them to overcome their anxieties and torments *before* being reduced to a state that obliges them to consult a psychiatrist? If they were given true knowledge they would not need to consult anyone.

But who thinks of giving human beings the knowledge that would enable them to develop harmoniously and to face any inner or outer difficulties? They have to fall ill before anyone will intervene. When they no longer know whether they are coming or going, when they are on the verge of suicide – or have already attempted it and failed – then someone hastens to reassure them, saying they will help them to recover peace, equilibrium and the meaning of life. In the meantime, they stuff them with drugs. Of course, when things have reached such a grievous state there is no other solution. But how long are we going to wait for people to fall ill before anything is done for them? You will say, "But that's science for you!" No! That is only a few crumbs of knowledge. Science, true science, is quite another matter.

True science will come into its own only when science and religion decide to work together to study those centers – those organs or instruments if you prefer – which enable human beings to establish communications with the spiritual world, the divine world. How can anyone imagine that the Creator, who has endowed human beings with all the instruments necessary to live and work in the material world, would leave them ill equipped to live and work in the spiritual world? The problem is that scientists will never venture along this path until the clergy is no longer content to present religion as a set of rules and regulations, the foundations of which are far from clear.

The splendor of churches and cathedrals, the brilliance of religious ceremonies, the beauty of the prayers and hymns kindle certain emotions in human souls, but this is not enough. People need something more definite than emotions and sensations, for emotions and sensations are short-lived, they do not provide a firm foundation for life. Even the faithful end by doubting, since they never try to go beyond the superficial notions that were perhaps sufficient in previous centuries, when people did not have the need to understand that we have today. So these "believers", while continuing to believe that they believe, are in fact "doubters". Contemporary human beings need to know, to understand, before they can really believe. The day has long gone when one could tell the faithful that the measure of true faith was to accept revelations they did not understand. They no longer want to hear about "the mysteries of faith". More and more they are going to reject these notions which they see as a form of slavery and a hindrance to their full development.

The progress mankind has made in scientific knowledge necessarily brings with it a change of attitude toward religion and, consequently, toward morality. Today, human beings need to understand that religion and morality are based on laws which are just as real and just as readily demonstrated as those that govern the physical world. For, as the universe created by God rests on certain laws, so the human beings created by God possess a physical and psychic organism which is also governed by laws. You all know from experience how easy it is to ruin your health. Perhaps you will say, "Yes, but medical science has made such strides!" True, medicine has progressed tremendously, but in spite of that progress, as long as human beings remain ignorant of the science of life, medicine will be powerless. For while medicine is trying to heal some of their illnesses, the disorders people continue to foster in their organism will only engender new ones.

If you puncture a rubber ball, a dent will form on one side, and however much you push at it to try and get rid of it, it will always pop up elsewhere. Similarly, I can tell you that although medicine has already made tremendous advances and is now making even greater ones, this will never enable human beings to live according to their whims and fancies. And no psychologist, no psychiatrist or psychoanalyst, will ever be able to restore the balance of those who break the laws of the moral and spiritual worlds.

None of the advances science has made in any field would have been possible if human beings had not understood that the physical world is governed by certain laws, by thousands of laws. And are they now telling us that the psychic world is a world of utter confusion, of total anarchy? That there are no laws that need to be known, no rules to be respected? No! That is impossible... If, through irresponsibility and lack of consciousness, human beings misuse the extraordinarily delicate mechanism of their psychic organism, they cause irreparable damage. One can count on nothing stable or dependable if the laws are not respected, because it is they that constitute the framework of the universe, the framework not only of the physical but also of the psychic universe. The greatest mistake human beings can make is to fail to recognize these laws. People behave as though they were a human invention, as though the principles on which they are based were arbitrary and open to discussion, as though they could easily be contravened. That is false! And let me say again that our understanding of things depends on the kind of life we lead. Knowledge can never be divorced from the way of life. Only a life of harmony lived in accordance with the laws of the cosmos makes genuine knowledge possible.

Religion is based on laws which govern the psychic life of human beings. This is why scientists must recognize the legitimate province of religion and understand that, since the spiritual life rests on laws, a science of the spiritual life must exist. I call on them, therefore, to broaden the range of their investigations. In doing so they will begin to see that their own discoveries actually confirm the truth of initiatic teaching; otherwise, whatever new discoveries they make, they will always be dissatisfied, for those discoveries will always be external to them. New discoveries may give them new ways of acting on matter, but one can have every possible way of acting on matter and still have a sense of inner emptiness. Scientific and technical discoveries do not nourish the soul and spirit.

Spiritual work is a long-term undertaking, but those who embark on it link themselves every day to the world of principles. They find meaning in it, and it is this meaning that gives them faith. Faith and also peace... It is not really possible to explain this with words, for it is a reality which belongs to a different dimension, but those who experience it cannot doubt their senses. Sometimes, very unassuming and unsophisticated people who have little book-learning can, by means of their inner research, know more about life than the greatest scientists. This is one reason why scientists would do well to show a little more discretion and humility. The Creator has not favored them with a special gift of knowledge. They may manage to control matter, but they cannot control life, because life cannot be found at the end of a scientific instrument, but within oneself.

You can journey to other planets and still be as earthbound as though you had never left home. It is all a question of your state of consciousness. What is the good of exploring the universe if one remains as inwardly limited as someone who has never ventured out of his native village? An astronaut can travel through space in his spaceship, but perhaps the shepherd who watches over his flock in the mountains and gazes at the starry sky in the silence of the night knows more about immensity than the astronaut. And if you say, "But that is not scientific..." you are wrong. Nothing is more scientific than what I have just been saying. And nothing is more useful. But it is a different science; one that is superior to any other. You do not believe me? Well, have it your own way... I am not asking you to believe me, only to do some experiments. Since you claim to be scientific, you could at least adopt a scientific attitude, that is, test things before drawing conclusions. Scientist do not begin with a certitude, they begin by experimenting, and they are ready to wait however long it takes to reach a conclusion. What does that make you, if, without any experimentation, you are content to declare that you do not believe me?

5

FAITH ALWAYS PRECEDES KNOWLEDGE

If spiritualists are often considered to be dreamers or even slightly demented, it is because their convictions are based on the invisible, on something that has no apparent reality. People think that anyone who claims to be rational should consider as real and trustworthy only those things that can be seen and touched by the sense organs, or indirectly by instruments capable of exploring and acting upon matter. Well, such rational people are simply ignorant. They do not know that the things we can see and touch are not reality. They are only external forms, only crystallizations produced by realities that are invisible, by forces, currents and entities. True reality cannot be seen or touched.

Reality... what exactly can we know about it? Reality is *our* reality, the level of consciousness we have managed to attain and which gives us a certain perception of people

and things. You will say that when we speak of
reality, we mean something objective, something external to ourselves, something that
everyone can see in the same way. Yes, this
appears to be so, but that appearance is
deceptive, for all supposedly objective reality is
necessarily transformed by our subjectivity in
order be touched, felt and known. We can never
be totally cold, unfeeling mirrors of reality; it is
impossible. However great our desire for
objectivity, we always shape and influence
reality; we always add or subtract something
from it. Subjectivity always has the upper hand.
Put several painters in front of the same
landscape and all their pictures will be different,
because certain psychic factors prevent them
from all seeing the same thing. So, when we talk
about reality, we can never be quite sure of what
we mean.

How much can we know about a human
being? We can describe and touch the physical
body, but we can neither touch nor describe the
entity which formed and now inhabits that body.
Matter gives us some indication of reality, but it
is not itself true reality. This is why, if you want
to change an aspect of your physical body, for
instance, it is no use trying to act on it, because
it is not true reality, but only a consequence. It
is the feelings and thoughts behind it which are
the reality, and behind these again, the spirit,

which has the power to fashion the body by means of thoughts and feelings. It is to them, therefore, that you should turn your attention so that they influence this form, your physical body, which will gradually be transformed and start to obey you.

We cannot see life, only the manifestations of life. We cannot see thoughts and feelings, only the various ways they express themselves in the actions and creations they inspire. In the same way, the world we know is no more than a physical condensation, the envelope, the cast-off crust of the invisible Being which vivifies, rules, illuminates and moves the universe. *What is seen,* says St Paul, *was made from things that are not visible.*[1] It is time human beings abandoned the old philosophies of unreality which keep them mired in the swamps of beliefs and illusions, and attached themselves to true reality: the spirit.

In spite of the lengthy studies and hard work involved, it is easy to deal with things we can see, hear, touch, taste and feel with our physical senses. To see, hear, taste, feel and touch things on the spiritual plane is much more difficult. And it is because human beings experience their inner world as a void into which they are afraid to venture that they cling to external objects and

1 Heb. 11, 3.

achievements. But fear is not going to get them anywhere. They must start by studying, learning the laws, and training themselves, and then they can leap into that "void", confident that they will neither lose their way nor fall. For, in point of fact, the void does not exist. It is the inner world which has not yet been explored that people think of as a void, but gradually, as one explores it, it is in that void that fulfilment is to be found. The only void that is a real danger to human beings is that into which they will inevitably fall if they believe that salvation is to be found in matter.

Faith puts us in touch with an unknown, infinitely great universe. St Paul also says that faith is *the conviction of things not seen.*[2] It gives us access to this world in which we can begin to breathe, to be nourished and strengthened. Little by little, realms hitherto unknown become familiar to us... we *know*. This is why we should never set faith up against reason; the two go together. Faith opens a path to new knowledge. One could say that faith is infinity, and in that infinity knowledge sets apart a very restricted area for itself. It is faith that sounds the depths of infinity, that explores it, that links us to it and allows us to penetrate ever further into its depths. In this way our

2 Heb. 11, 1.

knowledge of the divine world grows and is enhanced thanks to our faith.

Faith always precedes knowledge; it is faith that enables us to advance. In order to know, we first have to believe, and once we know, we no longer believe, and our faith carries us forward toward something we do not yet know. When we know we no longer need to believe; we have gone beyond it. And this is how, little by little, we achieve perfect knowledge, the knowledge that Jesus described as eternal life: *And this is eternal life, that they may know you, the only true God.*[3]

Faith precedes knowledge, then, and as we progressively acquire more knowledge, it strengthens the foundations of our faith. Only a faith based on true knowledge remains unshakable and enables us to continue to advance. As long as the foundations of his faith are not firm, there is always a danger that a believer will one day reject all of it or lose himself in a distorted form of faith. More and more today this is the great danger for all those who tend to confuse faith with occultism and who dabble imprudently in the invisible world, in an attempt to contact and make use of the forces which animate it, the currents which flow through it and the beings which dwell in it.

3 Jn. 17, 3.

This is why I warn those who claim to help others through clairvoyance and divination, or to heal their physical and psychic ills by magnetism, the laying on of hands, and so on. Very few people are allowed to have access to the invisible world so as to see the past, present and future, or to make contact with psychic and spiritual forces and entities in order to work with them. Why? Because the qualities one needs for this work are even more difficult to acquire than those needed for work on the physical plane.

It is not enough to have some psychic gifts – with a little practice, many people can acquire these. You must also have a high degree of self-mastery to ensure that, come what may, you always respect the rules of purity and self-lessness which alone give access to the luminous forces and entities of the universe. What will be the outcome if you have never wished – or never managed – to practice the discipline that demands a constant effort? Instead of enlightening and healing people you will deceive them and leave them weaker than before. Oh yes! The invisible world is well guarded. and those who try to force an entry will reach only the lowest regions... and then they had better look out! For not only will they suffer, but they will also be held responsible for the harm done to the lives of others.

Your faith must be founded on knowledge, and this knowledge includes a knowledge of the laws. A true materialist who rejects the reality of the invisible world is preferable to a self-proclaimed spiritualist who ventures into a world he knows little of with the intention of exploiting it for his own benefit, or simply from vanity, to attract attention to himself. In doing so he is breaking the laws of the spiritual world and sooner or later will have to pay for his transgressions.

Those who say they have faith must expect nothing more from it than a transformation, a perfecting of their inner life. Anything that is foreign to this consideration is not true faith. The knowledge accumulated over the centuries by the initiates was not meant for the use so many people put it to – the curious, the cranks, the sick and the crooks. What is needed now is for scientists to explore the faculties that enable human beings to relate to the world of invisible realities, and for this they will have to be ready to devote serious study to the experiences of spiritual Masters and great mystics. For, contrary to what many believed in the past – and continue to believe – true mystics are not those who launch into all kinds of fanciful flights of the imagination which lead nowhere. True mystics know where they are going.

It is obvious that the initiates of old could

not have the same knowledge of the anatomy and physiology of the human body as present-day biologists. But their practice of meditation and disassociation from their physical bodies made them aware that over and above the organs – stomach, lungs, hearts, brain, etc. – that enable them to live on the physical plane, human beings have subtle, etheric centers which enable them to be in touch with the spiritual world and to gain absolute certainties from their exploration of it.

Generally speaking, people are accustomed to dividing the physical and the spiritual worlds, but the truth is that there is no division, no break between the two, only a gradual progression from the physical to the etheric plane, and further still to the astral, mental, causal, buddhic and atmic planes. And the agents of this progression are the centers and organs which are, on the subtle planes, an extension of the physical centers and organs. You could say that these centers are transformers which make it possible for human beings to live harmoniously on the physical, psychic and spiritual planes at the same time, for there is a continual coming and going between them. This is true spiritual alchemy: the gradual transformation of raw matter into fluidic, etheric, spiritual matter and, conversely, the diffusion of that spiritual matter throughout the physical body which is thus quickened, vivified and regenerated. Hindu mystics call these centers *chakras* and situate them on the path of the currents that flow along the spinal column between the sexual organs and the brain. I have often spoken to you about the solar plexus and the Hara center, as well as the aura, which are also extensions of our physical body on the subtle planes.

Since the structure of all human beings is identical, it is possible for everyone to do this alchemical work. If very few actually do so, it is because very few are aware of the possibility, while still fewer make up their minds to buckle down to it. Most people are interested only in the ever more highly perfected instruments which science and technology continue to produce for their comfort and convenience – or their amusement. The instruments the Creator has given them with which to explore the world of the soul and spirit – a world infinitely richer and more beautiful – are neglected. They make use of only a tiny fraction of their faculties, the intellect, and as the intellect is limited, the horizons that open up before them are very narrow.

If science and technology have reached their present stage of development which is so greatly admired by all, it is because human beings possess spiritual and psychic instruments which serve as archetypes for those they manufacture on the physical, material plane. If this were not so, no amount of study or research, no reasoning could have led them to make such discoveries. Photography, for instance, is simply an end product of the history of the eye. The telephone, radio, radar, computers... all these instruments exist also within man. The brain itself is at the same time a telephone, a radio, a television, radar and a computer.

When we hear about scientific research our imagination conjures up a picture of people in laboratories working with various instruments and covering sheets of paper with their calculations. Well this is true enough, but if you were to study the case in depth, you would find that their unconscious mind plays a large part in their discoveries. To begin with, many have no clear idea of what they are looking for. They are simply motivated by the faith, the certainty that by searching in a certain direction they will find something. In a sense, they too are taking a leap into the void. Faith is present and acts as an antenna, a radar capable of discerning distant realities. There is a hint of something living, of a phenomenon... they have a premonition, a sensation, and that sensation cannot be denied. The heart (we can call it the "heart" since we are speaking of sensations) is capable of sensing things that are still hidden to the intellect. And it is these sensations that the intellect then studies.

As long as you sense nothing, as long as you have not lived, the intellect has nothing to work on. Yes, it is the heart, the capacity to experience sensations, that supplies the elements for science to work on. And the constancy and intensity of the efforts researchers deploy in their work sometimes bring them to the threshold of disassociation from their bodies. They find themselves launched into unknown regions, regions whose existence they had never imagined. This is why, all of a sudden, when they least expect it, a solution will come to mind. For others, a solution will come to them in their sleep: they wake suddenly, make a note of something and then sleep again... In the morning they can barely remember what happened.

Our souls travel and make contact with other worlds without our knowing it. And researchers – yes, even those who, claiming to be "scientific", deny the existence of this world of the soul, never having found it on the end of their scalpel, their microscope or their telescope – even they have souls which travel, make new discoveries and return from their travels with new knowledge. Naturally, if you question such people, they will say that they discovered something by pure chance. No! There is no such thing as chance. There are always certain preliminaries which lead them to this so-called chance.

Others have had an intuition about a discovery. They have sensed something and seen it with their inner eye without being able immediately to interpret or adapt it to the physical plane, without knowing how to put all the different elements together to make it work. And then, one day, they suddenly find the answer, and their intuition is confirmed. Whether scientists be atheists or believers, therefore, given the fact that their research work corresponds to a natural psychic process, it triggers certain mechanisms, and everything else follows automatically. Through their efforts of the will and of the mind, they activate certain forces, and once in motion, each force produces results, new discoveries.

There are thousands of scientists at work on research in the world, and their numbers make them a powerful force. It makes no difference that they do not believe that their research produces vibrations and waves on the mental plane which spread throughout the world; the results are there. Of course, it would be far better if they accepted this reality, if they were conscious of it. Their work would be easier, and they would no doubt be more inclined to undertake research that might aid the evolution of humanity. If they knew that the phenomena they study on the physical plane are analogous to those that exist in human beings, they would perhaps begin to take an interest in that prodigious equipment which enables the individual to work on the material of his own thoughts, feelings and desires, and on his states of mind. Not only would a vast and infinitely rich field of investigation be opened to them, but they would become true benefactors of humanity. Whereas now... just look at the situation of all those scientists who have seen their most marvelous inventions used for harmful, destructive purposes. Even Einstein came to regret that his work had contributed to the construction of the first atom bomb.

The realm of thoughts and feelings, the realm of human consciousness, this is what science must explore in depth. These are the breeding grounds of marvels, but also of unimaginable horrors. It is this that is real, although nothing can be seen. This is why the psychic world is the primary subject of study of all true initiates, of all who are truly wise. In this area, where nothing can be seen, they are firmly convinced that something exists, simply because it is so, because there can be no possible doubt. Sooner or later the results will be visible on the level of manifestation.

Those who undertake a genuine inner work are upheld by a growing conviction that they can never be deprived of the discoveries they are making or of the results they have obtained.

Whereas one can very easily be deprived of electricity, the telephone, a car... all those things of which the 20th Century is so proud – and justifiably so.

I am not asking for science to stop its research; on the contrary, what I wish is that it continue but in a different direction. Since the universe is a whole, since each human being is a whole, it would be true to say that science is seeking the same certainties as religion – although by other means – and that it will gradually come closer to the truths discovered by the great spiritual Masters of humanity.

6

RETRIEVING LOST KNOWLEDGE

A balloon is held captive by a string. It strains to rise toward the heavens, but it is tied to the earth. And, like balloons, we too have something within us which aspires to rise, to fly away, but which is held down by its bonds. It is these bonds that we must try to loosen, so that this profound, eternal aspiration engraved in the depths of our soul, this yearning to fly to the immensity of light and peace from whence we come, may be fulfilled. It is from this memory of a distant homeland – a memory which is often confused and vague – that we draw our faith, for we bear within us, in the depths of our unconscious, an indelible trace of that far distant past when we dwelt in the bosom of God.

If you question people, a great many will tell you that they believe in "something or someone", but they are unable to say exactly who or what. What they express in this way is both a feeling and an indefinable certainty.

Their intuition tells them that they once knew and experienced something, and occasionally, like a brief flash of light coming from the depths of time, that knowledge, that past experience rises to the surface of their consciousness. They have the impression that once, long ago, they knew something essential. They cannot remember what it was that they knew or experienced, nor do they know why the impression is so strong, but they cannot doubt the reality of it.

Sooner or later in the course of their existence, all human beings – unless they are monsters or complete brutes – have this sensation that something within them links them to a higher world, a world which remains mysterious but which has left its mark on them. The only difference between individuals is that some let this feeling fade without attempting to examine it more closely or reflect on what it might mean, whereas others make this inner conviction the starting point of a quest that leads them to the Godhead, the foundation on which, little by little, they build their faith. Thus faith is the result of an age-old knowledge buried deep within our subconscious. Those who never allow an echo of this knowledge to reach their consciousness will of course declare themselves to be non-believers. If they left the way open for currents flowing from the divine Source, they would recognize the presence of an immortal spirit and the existence of the higher powers.

One also meets people who, although declaring themselves to be non-believers, atheists, immediately add that they regret it, that they envy those who have faith. They never go any further; they behave as though to have faith or not were something that was completely independent of their will, as though faith were a talent, like a talent for mathematics or music. Either you do have the gift or you do not, and if you do not you may regret it, but there is nothing you can do about it. They are wrong! They do not really know what faith is; they confuse it with belief. Because they cannot believe any of the stories of creation, because they cannot believe in the existence of a God in heaven whose main occupation is to watch them, listen to their prayers and pass judgment on them after death, before sending them to heaven, hell or purgatory... Yes, because they cannot believe any of this, they are convinced that they do not have faith. But none of that is faith! Faith is a crystallization of knowledge that comes from the past. It is founded on an experience of the divine world, an experience which leaves indelible traces on every single being.

It is precisely because these traces exist within them that such people regret their lack of faith; they sense that something essential is missing. But if they do nothing to recapture that something, they will continue to suffer more and more from that lack. Even the greatest musical or mathematical geniuses would have achieved nothing if they had not worked... worked unremittingly. So it is no good thinking that one will find faith through a sudden gift of divine grace – which may or may not be forthcoming. It is impossible!

You probably wonder why it is that faith is self-evident for some people and not for others. The reason is simple: each human being that comes into the world brings with him the sum total of all that he has experienced in previous incarnations. All that he studied and verified for himself in his past lives is recorded in his soul and it now reveals itself as faith and an intuitive knowledge of the divine world. If today he acknowledges the existence of his heavenly Father, it is because he has known him and been in communion with him for a very long time, and that experience has left such a powerful impression on him that he can no longer doubt. Faith in God is engraved in his very being: he knows. This is why I have said that faith should not be seen as opposed to knowledge. Faith is knowledge based on experience. Those who have had experience of the inferior regions of their being in the course of previous incarnations draw conclusions from these experiences which naturally they consider to be the truth. So they too have a kind of faith – or lack of faith, which after all is a form of faith! And those who have had experience of the superior regions of the soul and spirit also draw conclusions – but their conclusions are, of course, different.

You may wonder why so many people say that they once had faith but have now lost it. The loss of faith usually occurs in adolescence. At adolescence, children who have believed everything they were told about God and religion (in exactly the same way as they believed fairy stories) begin to think that much of what they believed is false, and the rest is of no interest to them, with the result that they reject all beliefs. But those who have true faith cannot lose it. Even if they reject the beliefs of their childhood and experience periods of doubt and skepticism, a deep-seated faith endures in the depths of their being. For a while other concerns may take priority – business interests, personal ambition, and so on – but if they make an effort to rid themselves of all the dross, all the useless burdens that weigh on them and darken their lives, they will find themselves once again immersed in the source of life. They will sense, once again, that they are children of God.

We have a great deal of work to do, therefore, to rid ourselves of all the thoughts, feelings, desires and interests that hold us down on the lower levels of being – the astral plane (the heart) and the mental plane (the mind). God knows how inventive the hearts and minds of human beings can be when it comes to presenting things in ways that suit them and making other people prisoners of their desires and appetites! Oh yes! And the mind is always ready to aid and abet the heart by providing arguments to back up its desires. This is why intellectuals – may they forgive me for saying this – however intelligent and capable they may be in certain areas, are often the ones who make the most mistakes. You will protest that they are intelligent... Yes, but unfortunately that kind of intelligence does not prevent them from making mistakes, because it lacks one essential factor: the intuition which enables one to grasp the reality behind appearances. A renowned scientist or an eminent philosopher can still make the most stupid mistakes simply because they have never made the effort to rise above the astral and mental planes to reach the causal plane.

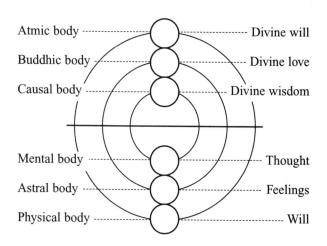

HIGHER NATURE

Atmic body	Divine will
Buddhic body	Divine love
Causal body	Divine wisdom
Mental body	Thought
Astral body	Feelings
Physical body	Will

LOWER NATURE

What is the "causal plane"? As I have often explained, the psychic and spiritual life of a human being resides in several different bodies, as illustrated in the accompanying diagram.

The causal plane – also known as the higher mental plane – represents the "rock" to which Jesus refers in this passage from the Gospels:

Everyone then who hears these words of mine and acts on them will be like a wise man who built his house on rock. The rain fell, the floods came, and the winds blew and

*beat on that house, but it did not fall,
because it had been founded on rock. And
everyone who hears these words of mine and
does not act on them will be like a foolish
man who built his house on sand. The rain
fell, and the floods came, and the winds blew
and beat against that house, and it fell – and
great was its fall!*[1]

Those who want to build a house must first
make sure that the land is solid, otherwise the
house will sink into the ground, the walls will
crack and the roof will fall in on those who live
in it. The house in the parable represents a
human being. If you base your existence on
sand, that is, on unstable ground that can be
shaken by chaotic thoughts and feelings (rain,
floods and wind), you will always be indecisive
and will end by collapsing. To stand up to every
kind of storm – both from within and without –
you must build your existence on the rock that
represents the causal or higher mental plane.
Only then will you possess true faith.

Faith, therefore, is a virtue which belongs to
the causal plane, the plane of active spiritual
forces. As the name "causal" indicates, it is here
that arise the currents that influence the mental,
astral and physical planes. This is why the work
we do when we rise to the causal plane has

1 Mt. 7, 24-28.

repercussions on our thoughts and feelings, on our everyday behavior, and even on our health. It is as though orders were given from above to organize and harmonize every aspect of our being. And progressively, as we experience these beneficial effects, our faith becomes stronger and more active, for what we are experiencing is the power of the spirit.

Unfortunately, human beings attach too much importance to theory and not enough to practice. It is time for them to make up their minds to practice, to apply what they have been taught, without always asking "Why? – How? – Will it be any use?" It is time to practice, to act... that is all. Try to experience that faith is the ground on which you must build your house, that is, yourself. Without this you will have nothing firm to rely on and will be exposed to every sort of misfortune. In any case, there will always be ups and downs; that is normal. Everyday life is full of surprises and unexpected events which may upset you and throw you off balance momentarily, but you must never let your faith depend on factors that belong to the astral or mental planes. If you do, one day you will believe because you feel well and happy, and the next you will doubt, because something unpleasant has upset you.

Faith must not depend on circumstances. If you have faith you will not be deeply disturbed by difficulties or failure; you will not complain that God has been deaf to your prayers for help and protection. You must be sure to react as soon as you sense some inner turmoil. Never give in to it! Never let yourself be dragged down by negative thoughts. Whatever comes, do your utmost to maintain the link with that inner region that is beyond the reach of every misfortune.

If so many people say that their faith is often troubled by periods of doubt, it is because faith is a very elevated state of consciousness, and to remain on that level, one must not allow one's consciousness to be obscured by all kinds of inferior thoughts and feelings. Look at trapeze artists and tight-rope walkers: they move freely through the air, and their freedom comes from the fact that they refuse to be distracted by alien elements that would upset their concentration and send them hurtling to the ground. And the same applies to those who have true faith: if they wish to remain on the high ground where faith is self-evident, their consciousness must be free of all negative concerns and murky feelings. Only if this is so can they remain on the heights of silence and light. Otherwise they will fall back to the level of belief, and not only is belief powerless to protect them, but it leads them astray.

When we are at the foot of a mountain our

horizon is limited, but when we climb to the top we can see a great distance and discover the land spread out before us. Mountains with their bases and summits exist also in us. The base is represented by our minds and hearts, always busy with schemes which limit and cloud our vision and lead us astray. Even if these schemes seem to succeed for a time, it is very unlikely that, in the long run, the results will correspond to our aspirations. The summit, on the other hand, is the spirit which can see everything exactly as it is at a great distance; the spirit which guides us and reinforces our convictions. Yes, faith is a virtue of the spirit which, seeing things from far above, knows how they will evolve. The spirit tells us what is going to happen – and it is always right. Faith is knowledge, the true light that reigns at the summit where there is no room for variation; whereas obscurity, instability and uncertainty reign down below. Depending on their level of consciousness, human beings fluctuate between these two regions.

To have faith or not to have faith depends entirely on ourselves. To lose one's faith is to cease to trust the power of the spirit within oneself. To have faith is to give first place to the spirit, resulting in a harmonious, beneficial activity. This faith is like the sun which illuminates, warms and restores life. Examine your life, analyze the foundations on which you have built it, and you will see how many empty, illusory, useless things you find... Yes, the years go by and you are still waiting. None of what you looked forward to has materialized; you are disappointed and embittered; your hair grows white, your teeth fall out... nothing is achieved. At last, before departing for the next world, people realize – but by then it is too late – that they have based their life on unfounded beliefs and lies. And at this point, refusing to be lucid and to recognize their errors, they blame others. But what is the use of blaming others? Will that change the sorry conditions in which they find themselves? No! And cosmic intelligence will not be moved to pity by such arguments. It will simply tell these ignorant people: "Every human being who incarnates on earth is the repository of a timeless knowledge concerning his origins and his destiny. It is up to him to allow this knowledge to rise gradually to the surface of his consciousness, and for this, he only has to prepare the right conditions."

Before a chemist conducts an experiment he gathers all the relevant elements, and he knows not only that they must be chemically pure, but also that the experiment will be successful only if certain conditions of proportion, temperature, and so on are respected. This law applies equally on the spiritual plane. Those who endeavour every day to purify themselves, to have noble thoughts and feelings, to make their lives harmonious, are creating the conditions necessary for true knowledge, true faith, to come to light within them.

Many travelers speak with wonder of experiences they have had in the desert or on a mountain peak. Face to face with immensity, imbued with the pervading silence, they say that they had a revelation of a time and space which was not human time and space. They sensed a presence which was beyond all explanation, all comprehension, but which they were obliged to recognize as something real, as the only reality. In exceptional conditions such as these, one can indeed have such an experience, but are exceptional conditions always necessary?

The truth is that this presence sensed in the midst of silence can be experienced everywhere, wherever one may be. If a man fails to perceive it, it is because he is inwardly immersed in a region of noise and commotion, the region of instincts and passions, of dark and chaotic thoughts and feelings. As soon as he succeeds in quelling that tumult, the silence which replaces it has the power to propel him into another time, another space, in which the divine knowledge written into his being from all eternity gradually reveals itself to his consciousness, and nothing will ever again cause him to doubt.

I talk... I repeat... I insist... I keep coming
back to the same questions. That does not mean
that I am unaware of how difficult an
undertaking this is. Our goal is to seek the
perfection of the heavenly Father, which is
obviously very difficult, almost unattainable –
some would even say, ludicrous, outrageous!
And yet it is a reality. Since God created us in
his image it should not be utterly impossible.
Some have attained it. And since some have
attained it, it is unacceptable to say that others
cannot do the same. There is no such thing as a
human race which is naturally superior;
similarly, there is no such thing as a naturally
superior human being. The differences that exist
between individuals are in their degree of
evolution, for not all human beings have exerted
the same effort, not all have worked in the same
way. The truth is that everything that happens in
the world, all that human beings experience in
life, be it happy or unhappy, represents no more
than an episode in that single undertaking: to
express to the full the image of God. If no one
repeats this to people, how will they ever make
up their minds to work in this direction? All
education should accentuate this question so
that human beings may find that knowledge
buried within them.

I have no wish to defend any religion. I have
no wish to defend God – in any case, he does

not need to be defended. Do you really imagine that anything human beings do – even if there are billions of them – on this speck of dust called Earth can really upset him? What are they compared to the immensity of the universe with its myriad population of creatures, angels, archangels and divinities? No, the ones I wish to defend and encourage are human beings. Yes, human beings, because their lives will never have meaning until they discover the image of God within themselves and work to bring that image to life.

7

A RELIGION IS ONLY
A FORM OF FAITH

People who have been to school and learned to think for themselves have always been seen as a threat by the dominant element in society, whose foremost concern is to stay in power. When people are informed and have developed a critical sense, they do not accept authority unquestioningly. They always put forward contrary opinions or objections, and as they grow in autonomy and independence, they can become a threat to that authority.

Yes, many people will tell you this: if you want human beings to be docile and obedient, it is better they be kept in ignorance. And to back up this opinion they will quote some of the numerous examples from history. In many countries, once the population began to be educated, peasants and workers could no longer be kept under control; they started a revolution and massacred the ruling classes.

The same phenomenon has been seen in

whole countries which have been helped to
develop through the introduction not only of
schooling but of all the latest technological
achievements. After a while, when certain
events have triggered a call for independence,
they have obtained it by attacking and driving
out those who helped them to benefit from the
advantages of civilization. But, once freed of
their "oppressors", most of these countries have
been a prey to civil wars, for those who were at
last liberated began to massacre each other.

What conclusions should we draw from
these examples? That knowledge is dangerous
and people should be left in ignorance? The
question will remain unanswered – or inade-
quately answered – as long as people fail to
understand that at the same time that the
intellect is being developed through knowledge
and information, it is indispensable to nurture
and develop another factor: a moral sense. With
the increasing dissemination of scientific and
technological knowledge, more and more
people are in a position to cause harm. All they
need to know is there, within their reach. Given
a minimum of competence and effort, everyone
can have access to it. There are things which
should not be made available to people until one
can be sure of their selflessness, their moral
strength, their sense of responsibility – in other
words, until they have been educated... And this

is very difficult.

Why is it so difficult to educate human beings? Because true education comes from example, and unfortunately good examples are rare. You can tell people: "We are here to bring you schooling which will give you tremendous possibilities. But as these possibilities must be used only for good purposes, you must also learn to be honest, altruistic and generous." Yes, you can tell them this, but it is not enough. You also have to show that you practice what you preach. And as this is not the case, the question of education is simply forgotten, or if some are concerned about it, they are told: "What about you? Do you behave as you say we should? You're in no position to preach to us!"

Knowledge is certainly one the best things that exist but, like all good things, it can be dangerous if it is misused. In any case, if anyone feels threatened by the dissemination of knowledge it is certainly those in power. This explains why, although the Churches have done a great deal to promote instruction, they have at the same time attempted to keep the faithful ignorant in certain areas in order to maintain their authority over them. Whatever the religion, we have seen and can still see this tendency. Take the case of India: how do the brahmins treat the outcasts, even today?

I do not wish to go into detail about these

questions – it is the general idea which interests
me: the fact that certain social classes, including
the clergy, attempt to hold on to power and keep
people in a state of dependency by depriving
them of all awareness of their inner freedom.
For centuries, in fact, Christians were told that
to be pleasing to God they should consider
themselves unworthy sinners, that they would
be saved only if they were humble, docile, self-
effacing – ignorant, in other words, for
knowledge inevitably leads to pride. As if God
could enjoy seeing human beings, which he
made in his own image, hopelessly mired in
slavery and darkness... The truth is that the
Church was simply trying to preserve its
authority and its privileges. But then, no
situation, however firmly established it may be,
remains unchanged for eternity. New currents
are appearing today which are going to cause
great upheavals. People are going to recognize
more and more clearly the contradictions that
exist between religion and true faith, and they
are going to start asking questions.

Suppose a person tells you that he is a believer, and when you ask him what his religion
is, he says he is Catholic – or Protestant,
Orthodox, Jewish, Muslim, etc. Then, as you
continue the conversation, you begin to realize
that the religion he claims to belong to has no
real impact on his life. It is no more than a

mixture of vague notions and meaningless forms. It is something he was taught in childhood and he continues to repeat it as one repeats a lesson learned by heart. His beliefs do not correspond to anything profound or alive. But if you point this out to him, he will not understand and will get angry. How can you doubt his faith?

Ask someone else the same question, and he will tell you that he belongs to no religion. That his parents were Catholic, say, but that they did not practice their religion. They did not have him baptized and gave him no religious instruction. Then, as you talk to him, you recognize that he has a sense of the sacred, that he is motivated by a high ideal, by the most noble aspirations. He does not know how to talk about God, but he has a vague sense of a higher presence in the depths of his being and in the universe as a whole, and he is seeking ways to improve himself so as to live in harmony with that presence. This person may have no religion, but he has faith.

I have met so many people in my lifetime! And I have so often seen the same thing! This is why, contrary to what most believers think, I say that religion and faith are two different things. Religion is a body of dogmas and doctrines presented to believers as articles of faith. But to have faith is not simply to adhere to certain doctrines. It is not necessarily opposed to dogmas and doctrines but it goes further,

Consider the Christian religion. To put it briefly, one can say that it is based on the following principles: Jesus, the only son of God, second person of the Trinity, incarnated on earth for the salvation of human beings. Through the operation of the Holy Spirit he was born of Mary, a virgin, the only human creature who, from the first moment of her existence, was preserved from original sin. At the age of thirty, Jesus began to teach and work miracles in Palestine. At the age of thirty-three he died on the cross. Three days later he rose from the dead and went up to heaven with his physical body. At the end of time all human beings will rise as he did. They will leave their tombs and come before him to be judged.

There you have a summary of the principles of Christianity. Those who doubt them cannot call themselves Christian. Thousands of believers have died in defense of these principles – which, incidentally, never prevented them from living like perfect scoundrels, not to speak of the very bad example members of the clergy have given in the course of centuries. But if you question certain Christians today, they will admit that they find it very difficult to believe all that the Church teaches about the divinity of Jesus, his birth, resurrection and ascension to heaven. And if they have difficulty believing these doctrines, it is because in the first place they are in contradiction to all the laws of nature and, particularly in the case of the resurrection of the dead at the end of time, are even diametrically opposed to common sense. And yet these same people feel profoundly Christian, for they realize that the life, teaching and sacrifice of Jesus show him to be a supreme model.

Then there are those Christians who have some notion of other religions and are obliged to acknowledge that they are based on conceptions as lofty as those of Christianity. They wonder why they are asked to believe that their own religion is so much better than others. Is it possible that God sent us his son only once in the course of history, two thousand years ago? If this is so, who founded the other religions? Lunatics? Impostors? Are all those who practice them living in error? If they lead exemplary lives, do they not have just as much value in the eyes of God?

More and more people are troubled by these questions. I have met some who are truly tormented by them. I especially remember the daughter of a Protestant pastor who was so deeply distressed that she was on the verge of a mental breakdown. I had to spend several hours explaining to her that religion and faith were not necessarily the same thing, and that even if faith is usually expressed through the dogmas and rituals of a religion instituted by man, it can equally well express itself without them.

Naturally, being a clergyman's daughter, she had studied the Bible, and I asked her: "Do you remember the passage which says that God will write his law in the hearts of men, and then they will no longer teach one another, for from the highest to the lowest they will all know him?" "Oh yes," she replied; "It's in Jeremiah!"[1] Well, I am always astonished when I see how well Protestants know the Bible. For my own part I can seldom quote a verse correctly; in fact I often do not remember what book it is in. But then it is not enough to be able to recite the Bible by heart; you have to know how to interpret it. So I explained it to that good young woman: "You see, it says that God writes his law in the hearts of men. Not in the hearts of *some* men, but of *all* men. Try to understand that to have faith means to be capable of reading that law in your own heart and stop tormenting yourself about whether your faith corresponds exactly to what your father preaches."

Of course, it would be unreasonable to leave human beings entirely to their own resources on the pretext that they must read God's law in their hearts, because most of them are not yet ready

1 Jer. 31, 33-34.

to do so. To be able to find God's law in our hearts and read it correctly, we have to begin by putting our house in order, otherwise we shall find only our own illusions and obscure desires. This should be the function of the religions: to teach human beings how to read the law that God has written in their hearts. Instead of that, they are content for the most part to burden them with all kinds of doctrines they do not understand and which are no help to them in their daily lives. So what kind of faith can they have? There are people who are proud to say that they are unbelievers. Well, that is their business. Leave them to it! The problem is for those who say that they are believers and who are struggling with irreconcilable contradictions.

How can anyone believe that people's inner lives will be nourished with what they are taught as articles of faith? It is as though they were asked to believe in mathematical operations. It is just as abstract. How many Christians see the notion of one God in three persons as a living reality? And those who ask questions about it are told that it is a mystery! Fortunately they have this law that the Creator has written in their being, for it is this that enables them – if they seek sincerely – to find in their heart and soul the things that religion does not reveal. And why do the religions not reveal these things?

Because they – or more precisely those who represent them – are usually more preoccupied with safeguarding their authority than with enlightening human beings, even if they claim to be saving their souls.

The desire for privileges and powers from which others are excluded is an innate tendency of human nature. And there are so many ways to dominate one's fellow beings. If it cannot be done on the physical plane, it may be possible on the psychological plane. A great many ambitious, fanatical and rapacious people have used religion as a means to achieve a psychological and moral ascendancy which they could never have achieved in any other way. This is why we are obliged to acknowledge that religion has too often become a human institution which has nothing to do with faith. Further proof of this is seen in the clergy's persistent desire to persuade the faithful of the superiority of their religion. The result is that, all over the world, people are convinced that their own particular religion is superior to others, just as they believe that their country is superior to any other country. They barricade themselves within the confines of their religion just as they barricade themselves within the borders of their homeland – which, incidentally, often coincide. And with such beliefs they never cease to commit crimes and to sin against God – Christians as much as others! This was not the example Jesus gave them. But then, have they ever read the Gospel account of how he behaved toward the Samaritans?

When Jesus went from Galilee to Judea he had to go through Samaria, and the Jews were supposed to shun the Samaritans whom they considered to be pagans and idolaters. The Samaritans were equally hostile toward the Jews. One day, when Jesus was on his way to Jerusalem, he sent his disciples ahead to a Samaritan village to prepare a room, but the inhabitants refused to receive them. And the Gospel continues:

> *When his disciples James and John saw it, they said, "Lord, do you want us to command fire to come down from heaven and consume them?" But he turned and rebuked them, and said, "You do not know what spirit you are of, for the Son of Man has not come to destroy the lives of human beings but to save them."*[2]

On another occasion, when he was again in Samaria, Jesus had stopped to rest by a well, and when a Samaritan woman came to draw water, he asked her for a drink. The Gospel tells us that the woman said to him:

> *Our ancestors worshiped on this mountain,*

2 Lk, 9, 54-55.

but you say that the place where people must worship is in Jerusalem. Jesus said to her... The hour is coming, and is now here, when the true worshipers will worship the Father in spirit and truth, for the Father seeks such as these to worship him. God is spirit, and those who worship him must worship in spirit and in truth.[3]

When his disciples returned they were astonished to see him talking to a woman, especially as she was a foreigner, for this was against the Law.

Then there was the occasion when a Doctor of the Law questioned Jesus about the love of neighbor that men are told to practice in order to win eternal life. Jesus explained it with a parable:

A man was going down from Jerusalem to Jericho, and fell into the hands of robbers, who stripped him, beat him, and went away, leaving him half dead. Now by chance a priest was going down that road; and when he saw him he passed by, on the other side. So likewise a Levite, when he came to the place and saw him, passed by on the other side. But a Samaritan while traveling came near him; and when he saw him, he was moved with pity. He went to him and

3 Jn. 4, 20-24.

bandaged his wounds, having poured oil and wine on them. Then he put him on his own animal, brought him to an inn, and took care of him. The next day he took out two denarii, gave them to the innkeeper, and said, "Take care of him; and when I come back I will repay you whatever more you may spend." Which of these three, do you think, was a neighbor to the man who fell into the hands of robbers? He said, "The one who showed him mercy." Jesus said to him, "Go and do likewise."[4]

So it was neither the priest nor the Levite, representatives of the Jewish religion, whom Jesus cited as examples, but an ordinary man, a Samaritan in fact, member of a community to which, as a Jew, he should have been hostile because they still worshiped idols. If Christians took the trouble to meditate on these episodes recounted in the Gospels, they would understand better that true faith is a state of consciousness which goes beyond the narrow boundaries of a religion.

You will say that Jesus was not particularly tolerant, that the Gospels often speak of him denouncing the scribes, Pharisees and Sadducees. That is true, but exactly why was he so angry with them? Because they respected

4 Lk. 10, 30-37.

only the exterior aspects of the Law of Moses
and used their authority to oppress the people.
This is why he told them:

> *Woe to you, scribes and Pharisees, hypo-*
> *crites! For you tithe mint, dill, and cumin,*
> *and have neglected the weightier matters of*
> *the law: justice and mercy and faith. It is*
> *these you ought to have practiced without*
> *neglecting the others. You blind guides! You*
> *strain out a gnat but swallow a camel![5]*

Or again:

> *Woe to you, scribes and Pharisees, hypo-*
> *crites! For you lock people out of the*
> *kingdom of heaven. For you do not go in*
> *yourselves, and when others are going in,*
> *you stop them.[6]*

So what Jesus blamed them for was that
instead of being motivated by true faith, they
were content to "sit on Moses' seat." He even
went so far, one day, as to tell them, *Truly I tell*
you, the tax collectors and the prostitutes are
going into the kingdom of God ahead of you,[7]
and to them this was the worst possible insult.

The Pharisees and Sadducees were very
proud of their learning, especially as it was from
this that they derived their authority. When they
argued against Jesus, they constantly referred to
the precepts of the Law, as though Jesus did not

5 Mt. 23, 23-24.   6 Mt. 23, 13.   7 Mt. 21, 31.

know them. Jesus never quoted the Law when speaking to the people, but when he answered the Pharisees and Sadducees he quoted other precepts to justify his behaviour, showing that he knew the Law as well as they did. In other words, the Pharisees and Sadducees chose what suited them from among the rules given by Moses and neglected others which they found less expedient.

We have to admit that Christianity has behaved no differently in regard to Jesus' teaching – and it is the same with all religions. As time goes on they sort out certain aspects of their founder's teaching and suppress those they find inconvenient. At the same time, they add all kinds of doctrines, rules and practices which they invent because they seem necessary to uphold the influence they seek to acquire.

Whether it be physically or psychologically, the tendency that is most firmly anchored is the domination of others. And when an exceptional being full of selfless love comes to liberate human beings, there are always some who immediately deform his message in order to use it to enslave them all over again. There are a thousand ways to enslave human beings, and to impose certain beliefs on them is one of those ways. This is how all religions have become, to a greater or lesser degree, institutions which oppress the masses.

So Christians must not imagine that they are very much better than the Jews whom Jesus reproved. If he came back today he would reproach in the same way the long succession of popes, cardinals, bishops, theologians, and so on, who have ruled the Church for centuries. They were supposed to teach human beings how to find true faith, that is, help them discover and develop their inner resources and spiritual riches. Instead of which, most of them behaved as though the Deity were their personal property, declaring: "No salvation outside the church!" Well, that might not have been too bad, but only on condition that the Church gave a good example by putting spiritual principles above everything else. The truth is that the Church fell into exactly the same error as secular powers: it tried to become an empire and put the main emphasis on organization. Today, the outward structure of the Church seems to be magnificently organized, but within this structure so much is crumbling and falling apart.

For centuries Christians persecuted Jews on the pretext that they were responsible for the death of Jesus. But suppose Jesus came back. Would he be pleased to see what Christianity has become over the centuries? May Christians forgive me for saying this, but the spectacle that greeted him and the sermons he heard would remind him of all that he condemned in the scribes, Pharisees and Sadducees. Once again, therefore, he would raise his voice against this state of affairs, and once again there would be those who, instead of listening to him, would plot to kill him. Oh yes, this time it would be the Christians who put him to death or arrange to have him silenced.

Everything that happens on earth has its source, its roots on the higher plane, in the divine world. Nothing you build on earth can endure if you do not begin by making sure that it is based on the spiritual plane. This is true even for political and social institutions, and all the more so for an institution such as the Church. By striving to become a temporal power, it gradually lost that which gave the Gospel message such power. At the same time it began to multiply its doctrines and articles of faith, to such an extent that they ended by obscuring that message. It is often difficult to recognize the voice of Jesus in what the church teaches today.

One of the things of which all established religions stand accused is that they all become gradually bogged down in matter, and this leads to many errors and also to many lies. This is why the faithful never manage to improve things much, either in their own lives or in world affairs. Man's true power is in his spirit, not in matter. For my part I am as capable as anyone of admiring the beauty of churches and of the ceremonies that take place in them. But the truth of a religion cannot be measured by the wealth and adornment of its temples or by the magnificence of its priestly vestments. Besides, many monarchs have owned even more magnificent palaces, clothes and ornaments. Over the years, the Christian Church has been transformed into a kind of museum in which can be found the whole history of architecture, painting and music. True, there are many things to be marveled at, but they were once alive and now they are no more than vestiges, leftovers. There are too many vestiges – and the spirit is lost. It is normal for the spirit to manifest on the material plane in ways that are appropriate, but what we see today is not a manifestation of the spirit in matter; it is, on the contrary, matter that has engulfed and paralyzed the spirit. Where is that faith today? Where is the ardor, the devotion that made it possible to create such masterpieces?

For many centuries, the religion taught to Christians was capable of producing exceptional achievements in the field of philosophy and art, but it is no longer enough. You can see proof of this in the fact that the churches are empty, the clergy is less and less numerous, and most of those who call themselves Christians are incapable of telling you exactly what they believe. Also, it is not difficult to see that they understand very little of their sacred scriptures, the Old and New Testaments. They respect and even venerate them, and are convinced that the Bible was divinely inspired, but all those texts written so long ago no longer correspond to their mentality.

The founders of the great religions, the initiates of the past, spoke for their own times. True, there are a certain number of truths which remain valid for all eternity, but they still need to be adapted to mentalities which change with the times. To take them literally can only result in their becoming incomprehensible, even scandalous. Jesus himself said that he had come to prolong the teaching of Moses: *Do not think that I have come to abolish the law or the prophets; I have come not to abolish but to fulfill.*[8]

People speak of revealed religion as though, at a specific moment in time, God had spoken in order to make himself known and give his commandments, and consequently that what he said must be considered unalterable, that nothing could ever be added or subtracted. But God did not come to manifest in person. He made himself known through the agency of his

8 Mk 5, 17.

most enlightened and most worthy sons, such as Moses, Zarathustra, Buddha, Jesus, Muhammad and all the great spiritual masters, many of whom are unknown, for their names are not recorded. Every one of these intermediaries belonged to a particular culture at a particular time in history. What they said could not be absolute or valid for eternity. This is why God – who is love – continues to reveal himself through other sons, other intermediaries whom he never ceases to send to earth.

A religion is only a form of faith, and no form can remain forever unchanged. Christianity, which saw the light of day in the Middle-East, rapidly acquired elements drawn from the Greek and Latin cultures. These were grafted on to those inherited from the Jewish religion, which, in turn, had been influenced by the religions of neighboring countries such as Egypt, Mesopotamia, and so on. A religion is never born from nothing. It receives elements from those that already exist, and it in turn is gradually transformed as it spreads ever farther from its place of origin. The peoples of Africa, America and Asia who were converted to Christianity have all added to it elements of their own culture.

Whether we like it or not, religions change. Even if the sacred texts remain the same, the gap between what people read and their way of thinking and behaving keeps widening. It would not be reasonable, therefore, to struggle to keep the same forms of a religion for ever. Humanity evolves because evolution is the law of life. As time goes on, human beings understand things differently and have different needs. In our day, for instance, people's knowledge of the psychic life has made great strides, and they have acquired – or rather, *many* have acquired – a moral sense that was entirely unknown to previous generations. And this means that religious truths must be adapted so that they may continue to be a living reality for them.

You only have to see how the notion of God has changed. How was it possible to talk about God, this being that is beyond all comprehension, to primitive people who had no notion of the inner life? As it was necessary to use a language they could understand, God was said to have various human qualities, with strong emphasis, of course, on his power and his greatness. In this way he took on the traits characteristic of earthly kings: he was thought to be authoritarian, quick to anger, jealous, vindictive toward those who refused to bow before him and generous with gifts to his courtesans. What noble matters for the Creator to concern himself with! And as the population of the world has increased, can you imagine how much work he has? Who would want to be in his shoes? There are kings on earth today who spend their time in more intelligent, more useful ways.

This is why, in our day, you will find fewer and fewer people who are ready to accept the idea of a God who will punish them if they disobey him, or reward them if they do his will. But they will be far readier to understand if you explain the effect their thoughts, feelings and actions have on their physical and psychic organs. Whether or not they will act accordingly is another matter, but sooner or later they will be obliged to acknowledge that it is true.

With the advancement of scientific and technological knowledge, our contemporaries are compelled to learn that the universe as a whole is governed by laws. So even though the word "God" may no longer mean much to them, they can understand that there is a cosmic intelligence which has established laws, and that these laws which govern the universe also govern the physical and psychic life of human beings. One of these laws is that whatever a human being does is recorded within him, in both his physical and his psychic organisms. Yes, whether they be good or evil, all his thoughts, feelings and desires, all his acts are recorded on the physical matter of his being. In the long run, all the bad things he does manifest within him as a deterrent, a limitation; conversely, all his good deeds give him immense possibilities for development.

So this is what human beings must be made to understand, otherwise neither the Church, nor the Bible, nor any sacred books – be they translated into every language in the world – will help them to improve. You must not misunderstand me: I am not casting doubt on the veracity of the scriptures, but although their way of presenting things was perfectly valid for centuries, it is not effective today. It is within themselves that human beings must find a reason to respect the divine laws, within themselves that they must find their divine model.

So let this be quite clear! When we speak of "revealed religions", we must not imagine that God himself incarnated on earth or spoke to a particular person in history to reveal truths which must remain forever unchanged. No religion can present the immensity, the infinity of God. In each period of history there is a corresponding form of religion. Note that I did not say "a" religion, but "a *form*" of religion, for we do not need a new religion.

Faith must be built on unshakable foundations, otherwise its precepts will eventually be abandoned one after the other, no matter how hard their champions try to defend them. In fact, as is obvious today, once those precepts are out of touch with the times, they are inevitably abandoned. All those commandments, all those precepts that are no longer relevant are like empty dwellings; they have been abandoned and their inhabitants have gone to live somewhere else.

Believe me, I make no claim to bring a new religion, only to extend and delve deeper into teachings whose principles are very old and need to be adapted to our times. Human history is a succession of changes. Nothing can stay as it is, for life is a perpetual movement. One would like to think that this movement always represents progress, but unfortunately we are obliged to admit that it sometimes constitutes a regression. But whether it be progress or regression, nothing stays put. Generations of human beings follow each other, and even if change is more gradual in some civilizations than in others, once conditions are ripe no one can prevent it happening. There seem to be certain currents which seize those who are ready for them and who then become the conductors of change, and if they succeed, it means that the time was ripe.

Now, if you look at history, you will see that all innovators – in whatever area – began by being misunderstood, even persecuted. These innovators did not set out to disrupt everything; it was not they who made up their minds to destroy certain things and introduce others in their place. They appeared because conditions for change were ripe, because mentalities were evolving. And this is also true of religion. All religion must evolve, and Christianity is no exception. If it refuses to evolve harmoniously, it will be obliged to do so with ruptures and destruction.

My work, I repeat, is not to proclaim a new religion. There are already quite enough religions in the world. The question is to know how best to work at nourishing our faith. This is what we should be doing. And this is why I give you methods, that is, an attitude to adopt, a program to carry out. It is not our role to argue about the essential truths which have been known for thousands of years. We simply need to know how to work so that they may remain always alive. In true religion, all human activity must be taken into consideration: those that concern our physical life – breathing, eating, walking, sleeping, and so on – as well as those that concern our soul and spirit. And if I emphasize methods of work, it is so that no area may be seen as extraneous to religion, for a human being is a whole. This is the foundation on which we should build our faith.

8

OUR DIVINE LINEAGE

Many people think that it is a demonstration of their great perspicacity, intelligence and powers of reasoning, to say: "For my part I only believe what I can see. If God exists, why doesn't he show himself?" But how can they think that this is a valid argument? To say that one does not believe in God because one cannot see him is idiotic. If you could see him you would not need to believe. Do you say that you *believe* in the existence of family and friends or of the world around you? No! You can see them, and that is enough. Faith is, by definition, a belief in the invisible, not the visible. But all these "reasonable" people fail to reason this far. They are content with their conviction that they will always meet others as "reasonable" as they, who will commend them and join them in deriding all those who are so naïve and feeble-minded as to believe in God. And as for those who do believe in God – what do they actually believe?

Recently, some friends from Bulgaria told me a story which was going around in the Communist countries. When the first Russian astronauts returned from outer space, they were received with great pomp at the Kremlin, where Brejnev congratulated them and pinned medals on them in the presence of many ministers, generals and other dignitaries. After the ceremony, Brejnev drew them aside, and said, "Tell me honestly: did you see God up there?" "Yes" replied the astronauts. "Ah!" sighed Brejnev; "I thought as much." Not long after, the same men had an audience with the Pope in a grand assembly of Cardinals at the Vatican. Once again, when everyone else had departed, the Pope said to the astronauts, "There is something I have been worried about. May I ask you a question: When you were in outer space, did you meet God?" "No, we didn't see him," replied the astronauts. The Pope looked a little disappointed, but after a few moments, he murmured "Ah, I thought as much!"

Whoever invented that story was a good psychologist and very observant. He knows that basically both believers and unbelievers are equally uncertain. Unbelievers put off believing in God until he shows himself to them, whereas believers have still not understood that faith is not founded on visible proof.

To try to prove the existence of God with

rational arguments is fruitless, an exercise in futility. I too can produce logical arguments for his existence – "Whereas... Since... Therefore..." – but I can equally well prove that he does not exist. The more you try to prove that God exists the more you cause people to doubt. And if they are not ready to accept what you say, there is nothing you can do about it. You can cut them up in little pieces, grind them to mincemeat, boil them in a cauldron... they will not change. There is absolutely nothing you can do. It is they who have to open themselves; you cannot do it for them.

You will say, "But surely, if someone were to work miracles in front of all those unbelievers, they would have to believe in the great truths of religion taught by the Scriptures." Don't you believe it! At the most they might be impressed for a few minutes, just as they would be impressed by a conjurer, but then they would forget all about it. It is useless to try to prove the existence of God, and I do not intend to waste my time trying. My intention is to help you to achieve a level of consciousness in which the question simply does not arise.

The truth is that the question of the existence of God can be answered only by analogy. You have a father who is close by, but he can sometimes go away on a trip. In fact, one day he will go away and not come back. Does this mean that he does not exist? No. Even if he is no longer physically present, he is still there, but his presence is within you. Because he is your father, he has left indelible imprints within you in the shape of physical or psychic traits, talents and qualities – or defects. Well, the same can be said of God: we bear him within us in spiritual form. Because he is our creator we are impregnated with his quintessence. He has left fluidic traces within us, a whole network of filaments which link us to him and thanks to which we can always find him. There is no answer for those who say: "God does not exist... If he existed..." or "God is dead...". There is only one thing you can say: God has given human beings the power to bring him to life or to kill him within them.

Anyone who thinks he can find God outside his own being is condemning himself to a sterile quest. We have to stop thinking of God "objectively", as a being outside of ourselves. We must even stop picturing him as dwelling high above us in the heavens, whereas we are down here, separated from him by an unimaginable distance. Since God created us he is forever within us, just as a mother and father are within their child. And as we bear within us our earthly mother and father, so – even more so – do we bear within us our heavenly Father and Mother. As long as human beings refuse this understanding of things, it is inevitable that at some point in their lives they will begin to doubt the existence of God.

It is God that gave us life. It is he that makes it possible for us to express ourselves through thoughts, feelings, words and acts. And whenever we feel an impulse toward light, whenever we are inspired by selflessness, kindness or love, whenever we feel the need to surpass ourselves, to make a sacrifice, it is a manifestation of God's presence within us. So strive to reproduce these experiences and you will understand what it means to believe in the existence of God.

You may ask, "But has no one ever met God?" That depends what you mean by "met". There are those who will tell you that God visits them every day; that he talks to them, gives them advice, entrusts them with various missions, and so on. And here, too, there is nothing one can say. It is useless to try and convince people who imagine that God is concerned about the details of their everyday life, or that he comes to give them a mission to the planet or to the whole universe. An encounter with God... it is only true mystics who have spoken of such an event. They have told of experiences which were true encounters, but inner encounters. No one has ever encountered God exteriorly... and even if such a thing were possible, there is no certainty that it would do much good.

Here, too, we must proceed by analogy. You go out shopping, and in the streets and shops you meet a certain number of people. One could say that you meet them and they meet you: they see you walking, going first one way and then another, choosing fruit or vegetables at the market, and so on. But can one say that they have truly met you? No. It is not because they have seen you that they really know who you are. You know very well that you cannot be reduced to a physical form. The true "you" dwells within. This is the being that thinks and loves and wills. And this being – the true "you" – is not visible to others. Even you yourself cannot see it. But does this mean that you doubt its very existence? No. So you admit that you cannot even see yourself, and yet you want to see God! How unreasonable! You will say, "Well, even if my body is not exactly me, at least it proves that I exist. I can see that." Yes, and you can see God's body too: it is the whole universe and all its inhabitants.

So do not look for proofs of the existence of God where they are not to be found. Look for God within yourself, and you will realize that he is always there; that he never leaves you. If you cannot feel him, it is not because he is not there, but because you have turned away from him.

You have not been attentive to his presence, you have not been sensible, you have committed certain faults which have clouded your consciousness, and now you have sensations which mislead you about reality. God is always there, it is you who have allowed your awareness of his presence to be dulled, and now you must do all you can to recapture that presence.

There are children who have never known their parents and do not even know who they are. But they never doubt that they had parents – in fact, many spend their lives looking for the slightest clue to their existence. The truth is that their parents are within them, in all the quintessences they have passed on to them. Whether they are physically present or not, they are always present inwardly. Yes, children always have their parents with them, in them. Biologists and psychologists study children to see how the laws of physical and psychic heredity apply to them. This is good, but it is not enough. Who is there to study our spiritual heredity, all those divine seeds received from our heavenly Father and Mother, which we must cherish and develop until we resemble them?

The Book of Genesis says that on the sixth day, after separating the earth from the waters and creating the sun, moon, stars, plants and animals, God said: *Let us make humankind in*

our image, according to our likeness.[1] The
universe is the body of God, a body which he
animates with his spirit. In the same way, human
beings possess bodies which are a reflection of
the universe, and the spirit which animates these
bodies is a spark of the divine Spirit. So if you
wonder where God is, and you picture him as a
monarch whose throne is out of sight in the
farthest and most inaccessible corner of the
heavens, then you will certainly never find him.
No doubt, God is the most remote, the most
inaccessible being, but at the same time he is the
nearest, for he is within us.

We have much work to do in order to sense
that presence within us and give it life. Nothing
is more precious than the sensation of being
inhabited by the Creator, for whatever comes,
we can never doubt his existence again.

For centuries Christians and Jews have
repeated that God made man in his image. They
repeat it, yes. But do they really understand
what this means? In creating us, God placed
within us a quintessence of himself, a quintessence of the same light, the same purity and
the same power. It is this inner quintessence
that initiatic science calls the higher self. By
concentrating on our higher self, therefore, we
are linking ourselves to God, for that higher self

1 Gn. 1, 26.

is a particle of God. Thanks to our efforts to reach this center, this summit within us, we cause forces to flow which are capable of vivifying all the cells of our body. And this is God's answer to our prayers, for God is not different from our higher self.

We can touch God, the cosmic spirit, only insofar as we manage to touch the spirit within us, our higher self. You must understand, therefore, that when you are praying to God, it is really the summit of your own being that you are trying to reach. And if you succeed, you trigger a vibration of great purity and subtlety which, spreading throughout your being, produces extremely beneficial transformations. Even if you do not obtain what you asked for this time, you will at least have gained some very precious elements. Your prayers will have been productive in that by striving to reach the high point of your being, you have set a force in motion on a very distant, very high plane, and as it comes closer to you, it produces sounds, scents and colours and regenerates the whole of your being.

Instead of wondering where God is and what he is like, you would do better to work on the quintessence of himself that he has placed in you, otherwise you will be embarking on a fruitless quest. Philosophers have attempted to define God by saying that he is a circle whose center is everywhere and whose circumference is nowhere. Well, I have no objection to that, but with such vague indications, how can you possibly find him? Since he is everywhere, you must realize first and foremost that he is in you, and this means that you always have the possibility of meeting him, of talking to him and listening to him. It is he who wants to infuse himself into his creatures, so he is a part of you and you cannot lose him. If you lose him it simply means that you have not sufficiently realized that you possess him.

If so many people admit that they do not believe in God, it is because they have been content to accept what they were told about him, and what they were told remained external – just words. Words, even the truest and most profound, are always external, and this means that there is always a danger that they will lose their meaning. Only human beings can truly give them meaning, can truly preserve their meaning, and to do this they have to assimilate them and make them their own.

You cannot lose what you truly possess. You can lose only that which does not really belong to you, that which has not become fully a part of yourself. At one moment you believe, and the next you doubt; at one moment you are illuminated and the next you are in darkness; at one moment you love and the next you love no more. This means that neither faith, nor light, nor love belong to you. For them to belong to you, you yourself have to become faith, light and love. Jesus could say *I am the light of the world,*[2] because he identified with light. He did not say that light was in him or with him. He said that he *was* light. There is a world of science in that phrase which we must meditate on and put into practice in every aspect of our inner life. We can lose many things that belong to us on the physical plane. But that which is in us, joined and fused with our being, that which has become part of our own flesh and blood, cannot be lost. At this point we no longer question the existence of God, for how can we doubt what we are?

Faith is present in the depths of our being. God has written it there by his presence, and it only needs to be set free to manifest. We are inhabited by a faith which is absolute because God willed that we should be eternally linked to him. When a spiritual Master or initiate tells us not to sever our link with God, it is only a figure of speech. The fact is that it is impossible for us to sever that link, because we are of the same nature as God. The only thing that can be severed is something in our consciousness which can become shriveled or obscured. Our

2 Jn. 8, 12.

true self is never far from God, for God is in us as we are in him.

Perhaps you are wondering why, since we are of the same nature as our Creator, we feel so different from him. The answer is that in descending onto the material plane, we allowed too many opaque elements to come between our spirit and our ordinary level of consciousness. Human history goes back a very long way, and if we want to understand it, we must once again refer to Genesis:

> *In the beginning when God created the heavens and the earth, the earth was a formless void, and darkness covered the face of the deep, while a wind from God swept over the face of the waters. Then God said, "Let there be light."* [3]

And it was at this point that creation began.

As indicated by the terms "formless void", "darkness" and "the deep", the universe before creation was an expanse of chaos and darkness. But hovering over this chaos is the spirit of God. I have already explained to you that water is the symbol of the primordial matter which was fertilized by fire, the divine spirit, to produce fruits of great wealth. And as the spirit fertilizes matter, it also fashions it; new creations gradually take shape, and matter begins to

3 Gn. 1, 1-2.

discover its powers and to know itself. And now, if you ask me why God created the universe, I will answer: "In order to know himself." The Cabbalah teaches that God wishes to know himself through his reflection, and it expresses this idea as a stretch of water which reflects the visage of God. Of course, the question remains: *why* does God want to know himself through matter? But that is the mystery.

So God wants to know himself through matter, and this is why he created the sun and planets, the rocks and plants and animals – and human beings. And because human beings were created in the image of God, they too want to know themselves through matter. The human spirit is immersed in matter (in the body, which is a synopsis of the universe), and it seeks to know itself through that matter. But it will achieve this only after thousands and thousands of years, when it has labored to make that matter so subtle and transparent that it will be able to see through it. Until then the spirit cannot know itself; it is, as it were, estranged from itself, lost in the opacity of matter.

Throughout this arduous voyage through matter, our only salvation lies in faith, faith in our divine origin, in the assurance that we are on earth for one purpose only: to know ourselves as spirit so as to manifest the light and the power of the spirit. This light, this power dwell within us already; they are always in us and sometimes, in exceptional circumstances, we feel them breaking out. Then we believe that they have come from elsewhere, from who-knows-where... No, we have always possessed them within us, but it is only at this particular moment that we have made it possible for our spirit to manifest through matter.

Our spirit is omniscient and omnipotent, like God. It dwells in infinite, eternal light, but our brains are not capable of communicating this to us without interruption. Why not? Because the brain's ability to communicate to us the light, knowledge and powers of the spirit is related to all the other aspects of our physical and psychic life. You might try this experiment one day: from the first moment of waking in the morning until when you fall asleep in the evening, try to be aware of all the processes that keep you alive. All these physical, psychic, emotional and mental processes that are too numerous to name – it is through them that you are in contact with matter, that you work on the plane of matter. If you learn to watch what you are doing and to make sure that they all take place in the best possible conditions of purity and harmony, the functioning of your brain will improve as it gradually becomes a conductor for the powers of the spirit. This is the truth on which you should found your faith, and in this way you will become invincible. You will understand that nothing can undermine you or cast a shadow on you. Nothing can destroy you.

Through our spirit, our higher self, we are close to God, in God, and it is through him that we can tame our lower self. On the higher planes we are already free and dwelling in the light, and we must make this true on the lower planes also. The link between the higher and the lower planes, between spirit and matter, were studied in depth in initiations of the past which expressed them through various symbols.

One of these symbols is the serpent that swallows its own tail. The serpent's head represents our higher self, and its tail, our lower self. The initiates used this symbol to tell us: "You are in God, in the light, and at the same time you are outside him and in darkness." But the head and the tail belong to the same creature, the serpent, so they are not separated.

And since the serpent swallows its tail, this means that our spirit, our higher nature, works on our matter, our lower nature. It is our spirit which has to take control of our matter so that there shall be no contradiction between the two.

The same idea can be seen in the fourteenth card of the Tarot, Temperance. On it we see an angel holding a pitcher in either hand. From the pitcher in his left hand he is pouring water into

that in his right hand, and this water represents life, the current of divine life. If he were to interrupt the flow there would be no more exchange, and human beings would make no further progress. They would never attain perfection. As for the angel, he represents us. Yes, each one of us is the angel that has the power to work with the two pitchers. Whether or not the divine world, the spirit, comes from on high to animate, exalt and vivify matter below depends entirely on us. It is this descent that we are preparing when we strive to rise through prayer and meditation, for the downward movement can only happen if it is preceded by an upward movement. The spirit can come down only if we do the preliminary work that gives it the possibility. Every day, through prayer and meditation, we must learn to pour out that elixir, that heavenly quintessence, so that it may fill our whole being.

Another symbol which expresses the work we have to do is the Seal of Solomon. This is a figure formed by two equilateral triangles interlaced. The triangle with the apex pointing up represents the human being who, through his spiritual work, strives to attain the divine world. The other triangle, with the apex pointing down, represents the downward movement of the divine world, which seeks to impregnate the human being with its light. The flow of energies

between the two worlds is shown not only by the interlacing of the two but also by the fact that they communicate. Unity is the truth of creation. This is why matter and spirit must become one, thanks to their mutual relationship. The upper and the lower, the superior and the inferior must fuse into one, and in that fusion each is constantly enriched by the other. That which is inferior is absorbed by that which is superior, while becoming at the same time its material receptacle.

For centuries and millennia, initiates have taught this truth to their disciples, but depending on the peoples and civilizations concerned, their teaching has taken different forms. But even if this teaching – said to be esoteric or initiatic – were revealed to very few, all religions remind man of his divine origin and teach him ways by which he may become one with the Godhead. Religions are one thing, however, and their representatives are another. How many representatives of religion are truly dedicated to helping people become aware of their origins or to giving them the means to find the Deity in themselves? No wonder – in spite of the existence of sacred books whose elevation and beauty can never be surpassed – one sees so many people wandering off course and surrendering to the downward pull of forces which inhabit their inferior self. No wonder that, faced with such a spectacle of chaos, people say that God does not exist.

If so many so-called believers are obliged, at some point, to admit that they no longer have faith – or that perhaps they have never had it – it is because no one ever explained to them that faith begins by a knowledge of human beings and of the work we have to do on ourselves. Those who have already begun this work can no longer question the existence of God. They sense that they are linked to that existence, that they are a part of it. They can no more deny the existence of God than they can deny their own existence. Many people think that it is the ignorant who will be impressed by the knowledge of those who know, or that it is the wicked who will be impressed by the qualities of good people. Not at all! If you really want to know what stage of evolution people have reached, you must see whether they are capable of appreciating the worth and the virtues of others. If they are not, it means that they themselves are not worth much. One has to possess certain qualities in order to appreciate them in others. In the same way, in order to recognize that Being that surpasses all beings, to appreciate his wisdom, his perfection and his splendour, one has to have developed some of that perfection in oneself. We can perceive only that which corresponds to what we are.

When I say this I am only pursuing the idea Jesus expressed when he said: *The Father and I are one*,[4] or when he reminded the scribes and Pharisees of the Psalm which says: *You are gods.*[5] This is what true Christianity is. If you do not accept this you will never resolve the apparent contradictions in the Scriptures. You will never pierce their meaning. You will never learn to join the head to the tail.

We give ourselves a goal, and to reach that goal we have to follow a certain path and apply certain methods. But in reality, goal and methods are one and the same. When Jesus said, *I am the way, and the truth, and the life,*[6] he was identifying with the path, the way. He walked the path and he was that path. And those who follow Jesus, those who walk this path, must themselves become the path. They think about

4 Jn. 10, 30.   5 Ps. 82, 6; Jn. 10, 34.   6 Jn. 14, 6.

God, they advance toward God, and they themselves must become God. That is, they must identify with their goal. In this way the goal becomes the method. And the method comprises all the exercises which enable us to advance in order, one day to become one with God.

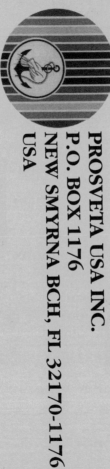

Buy Online at:
www.prosveta-usa.com

PROSVETA USA INC.
P.O. BOX 1176
NEW SMYRNA BCH, FL 32170-1176
USA

US Postage

OMRAAM MIKHAËL AÏVANHOV

Please Send: ☐ Catalog ☐ Newsletter

Name:_____

Address:_____

City:_____

State: _____ **Zip:**_____

Tel:_____

E-mail:_____

9

PROOF OF GOD'S EXISTENCE
LIES WITHIN US

I have sometimes been asked whether I believed in God. My answer was "No, I don't believe in God." What is the point of believing? What does it mean to believe in God? We must communicate with him, touch him, feel him, live him... then we have no need to believe... To believe supposes that the object of our belief is far away, that we have never felt his presence, never known him. Then, yes, we believe, but we do not really know why we believe, nor even what we believe in.

What many think of as belief in God is something feeble and undefined. Belief is for those who have never really felt anything at first hand. A person will say, "I believe," but it does not amount to much. We have to go further than that. Atheists, too, believe in something. In their own way, they too are believers. They believe that God does not exist. This too is a belief, but one which is of no benefit to them, for you cannot be nourished by something that does not exist. Doubt about the existence of God has no reality, it is inexistence, and that inexistence cannot truly be felt. Whereas it is possible to feel the reality of God – and not only to feel it, but to live it.

Whether believers or unbelievers, we all have our existence in God, and God lives in us. The difference is that the former are aware of it and the latter not. The unbeliever continually builds up internal barriers to the point where he feels nothing, and since what one cannot feel does not exist, he ends by saying that God does not exist. And that is absolutely true. In such conditions he does not exist. But for one who believes in God, he does exist. However, this belief is not yet fully conscious. For it to become conscious, the believer has to reach the point where he senses that God lives in him and that he lives in God, that he is indissolubly one with him. From then on, nothing can cause him to doubt again, for he lives the divine life continually; he is immersed in it; it pervades his whole being.

It is man who determines whether beings and objects exist for him or not. Suppose a person is asleep: the treasures of the whole world could be piled up around him, but as he is asleep he is completely unaware of them. It is as though there were nothing there. It would be true to say that the consciousness of most human beings is fast asleep. The initiates, on the other hand, who are truly awake, can see and be overawed by the splendours all around them. Others have the same treasures around them and in them, but they do not realize it. So everything depends on one's level of consciousness. When we are awake, certain things take on reality for us; then we sleep and they fade away. And the same is true for God: those who are asleep do not sense his presence and conclude that he does not exist. The example of sleep can be very instructive.

Researchers who have studied the question of sleep have found that it has several phases, several levels. Similarly, on the psychic and spiritual planes, there are several levels of sleep or wakefulness, that is, several levels of consciousness. Our task, therefore, is to awaken. The Christian tradition says that we must be born again. Why "born again"? This is the expression Jesus used when speaking to Nicodemus: *No one can see the kingdom of God without being born anew.*[1] But in reality, new birth, like awakening, is an ongoing process; every step forward on the path of light and of truth is a new birth, a new awakening. To be awake! Yes – in fact this is the meaning of the

1 Jn. 3, 3.

name Buddha: "the Awakened".

However much theologians and philosophers endeavour to prove the existence of
God – even though some of their arguments
may be very interesting – it cannot actually be
proved. At best one can tell unbelievers that the
most convincing proof is their own existence
and that of the world around them, but here too,
there will always be some learned men to
proclaim that man and the universe are the
result of chance. Ah! So there is a creator called
Chance! Well, there is nothing to be proud of in
this discovery. The truth is that these people are
asleep. And because they are asleep they are
incapable of appreciating the riches and
splendors that surround them. But even worse is
their inability to see all that they themselves
possess, all the gifts and talents, all the faculties
and possibilities which are a manifestation of
the Deity within them. Sleep is a form of
blindness: their eyes, their spiritual eyes are
closed.

The superior needs that express themselves
in human beings are a manifestation of the
Deity. It is by their lofty aspirations and their
activities for the benefit of others that human
beings witness to the existence of God.
Gradually, as their consciousness expands,
perceptions of another order reach them. It is as
though they were being infused with another

life, the life of that sublime Being, as though his inner presence were becoming more and more pervasive. By intensifying that presence they merge more and more with it, until one day they resemble the Deity.

The most cogent proof of the existence of God is to be found within. The Creator has placed seeds within each one of us, and the destiny of a seed is to sprout and grow until it becomes a tree. Remember the parable of the mustard seed... and remember that each one of you is a seed. In other words, you are all potential divinities, and it is through your work, through the higher manifestations of your life, that you will become divinities in reality. Otherwise you will remain as seeds – or perhaps as roots – but you will never be branches, leaves or flowers, still less, fruits.

It is only what you are that can prove the existence of God. But be careful: this proof is valid only for you. Even if you become a divinity, you will never prove the existence of God to others unless they too rise to such heights of consciousness that, in their dazzlement, they will be unable to stop themselves thinking: "What I have discovered is so beautiful, so luminous, it can only be the Deity!"

Some of you will say, "No one has ever talked to us about God in this way. What we

were told was so superficial, so puerile, so
ridiculous... we could not believe it, so we lost
our faith." But who obliged you to accept that
notion of God? Why deprive yourselves of
something essential simply because no one
knew how to talk about the Deity? Why do
human beings always need someone to talk to
them about the presence within them – within
all beings – of something, someone, infinitely
vast, beautiful, luminous and powerful, of
someone overflowing with love to whom they
must always be linked in order to give a
foundation and direction to their lives? If they
cannot sense this presence, it is quite simply
because they are asleep.

And now, how can we awaken human beings
from that deep sleep? Here again, a comparison
between psychic and physical sleep will help us
to understand. On the physical plane, someone
who has accumulated too many toxic elements
or debilitated his organism by an undisciplined
way of life will sleep very heavily. He will need
time to recuperate, and when he wakes he will
drag himself about, still half asleep. Similarly,
someone who accumulates impurities in his
heart and mind, or who drains himself of energy
by giving way to his passions, will be sunk in a
state of psychic torpor. It is this sluggish state of
consciousness that prevents him from sensing
God's presence within him.

Nothing is more real, more true, than the existence of God. The fact that it cannot be proved is actually an argument in its favor. If God were as we want him to be, if we could see and touch him, it would mean that he had limitations – in other words he would no longer be God. It should be enough for us to sense his existence without asking that it be proven by such limited, inadequate means as our five senses.

Whatever people tell you, therefore, and whatever philosophies prevail in the world, cling to this idea that you can find God only within yourself. Look for him. Think of him. Love him and call on him, because in this way you will receive the extremely potent energies that will enable you to advance unwaveringly on all the paths of life. Christians sing the Psalm: *The Lord is my shepherd, I shall not want. He makes me lie down in green pastures; he leads me beside still waters.*[2] Yes, but they repeat the words mechanically, automatically, not realizing that they are magic. This shepherd is within them, and because he is in them he extends his power and his protection to the immense flock of their cells, to whom he gives food and drink. Nothing is more important than the consciousness of the presence of God within.

2 Ps. 23, 1-2.

Thanks to this presence, thanks to the thought of this presence, everything becomes ordered and serene, everything falls into place and becomes harmonious and well balanced. And even if you do not achieve much in the way of visible results, it does not matter. You will at least have obtained the essential: you will be going forward on the right path.

Why are human beings weak? Why are they unhappy? Because they look for everything – even God – outside of themselves. But God is *inside* us. We cannot separate ourselves from him. At the most we can only put dark, opaque screens between him and ourselves. When the sun is hidden behind the clouds, it does not mean that it has disappeared; it continues to radiate its light and heat. And when the clouds move on, or when we rise above them, we can see that it is still there. An identical phenomenon occurs in us: like the sun, God is always there, present and immutable, sending us the light, wisdom and warmth of his love. But, of course, if we allow dissonant, selfish, malevolent thoughts, feelings and desires to build up into clouds within us, we will be deprived of that light and warmth. The trouble is that instead of realizing that it is their own fault and doing what they can to remedy the situation, people complain that God does not exist or that he has abandoned them.

There are times when even believers, even many mystics have felt as though God had abandoned them. As though it were God who changed toward us! Oh yes, it must be God who changes! We ourselves are always steadfast, always unwavering in our faith and love. It is God who is fickle! Sacred scriptures say that God is faithful and true, and although human beings repeat these words, they are forever wondering why God does not see or hear them, why he abandons them. But it is not God who abandons us, it is we who abandon him. How do we do this? Instead of rising above the cloud level, we sink below it, and there, of course, it is cold and dark. We should stay up above the clouds, up where cold and darkness exist no more, for it is there that God dwells, and it is there that we can dwell in him and he in us.

Perhaps you have never been up in a balloon, but you know what it is that makes a balloon rise: the heat generated by burning gas dilates it, making it lighter than air. Similarly, if we want to rise on the spiritual plane we also have to become light and dilated, and for this, something within us has to be heated. When the heat of love dilates our hearts we become so light that we begin to float upward like a balloon. So, as you see, we can learn more by knowing how to read the book of nature than by reading books of theology. The book of nature teaches you that if you grow cold you will contract and become heavy, heavier than air, and then you will fall to earth. And when you are on the ground, of course, you say that it was not worth believing in God, because he has let you down. But warm up your heart again, fill it with love, and once again you will soar up above the clouds to find the sun, the Creator.

Like the sun, God gives us all his blessings, but if we close our hearts to him we cannot receive them. In reality God does not need our love, but he has built human beings in such a way that they need to love him. That is, they need to open themselves so that he may enter them. If they refuse to open themselves or prefer to remain below the clouds, well that is their free choice. God lets them do it. You will say, "Yes, but he becomes angry and punishes them." Ah! Do you really think so? God has many far more important things to do than punish or reward human beings. It is they who, by their good or bad attitude, trigger a state of harmony or disharmony in their own hearts and souls, and it is this harmony or disharmony that makes them think either that God protects and smiles on them, or that he abandons and punishes them.

God is too great to be concerned about the errors or wickedness of human beings. And he is immutable. He does not change according to their attitude. So, when you feel anxious and troubled, when you feel lost in a void because you have behaved badly, don't say that God has withdrawn. It is up to you to make the effort to get close to him. If you do this you will succeed, and then you will find that he is not vindictive and unforgiving as people have so often said of him. So make the effort to repair your faults; don't wait until you feel that God has forgiven you. He has not condemned you and he has no need to forgive you. There is no point in beating your breast and calling yourself a sinner. Since it was you who manufactured the clouds that hid the light of God from you, it is up to you to disperse them. It all depends on you, on your attitude. What is the use of all the progress that has been made in psychology if human beings cannot understand and control such important phenomena that occur within them?

This idea that God comes close to us or moves away hinders our progress. You tell yourself: "God has withdrawn, so I'll wait until he comes back." Well, you can wait for centuries. No, it is you who must begin immediately to change this state of affairs. If you delude yourself by waiting for the change to come from God, and instead of acting are content to call on him to rescue his wayward child, you will only be prolonging your inner disquiet. Since it is you who are the cause of this disquiet, you must

make amends for your faults. This is the true
repentance that will bring you back to God. To
say that God forgives you is an illusion; we are
forgiven only if we make amends. As you see,
you need to free yourself from many false
notions encouraged by the religions themselves,
and whatever the circumstances, work to rise
above the clouds, so as to find the Deity within
yourself.

10

IDENTIFYING WITH GOD

It must have happened at least once in your life that you were listening to someone – a friend or a stranger – talking about himself, about his uncertainties, his hopes and sorrows. You listened closely and followed what he said with attention. At one point you felt sympathy, at another, astonishment, alarm, compassion or wonder, and yet, what he told you remained exterior to you. And then, suddenly, you had the sensation that you were in him – or he in you – and you realized that you truly knew and understood him.

Generally speaking, an experience of this kind happens independently of one's will. But since it can happen, it is possible to experience it voluntarily as an exercise in identification: identification with those we love and admire, but also with certain natural phenomena, with a river, a waterfall, a spring, a star, the blue sky, even the sun. Yes, you can contemplate the sun and enter into it, imagining that you yourself are the sun. You have no idea of the transformation you are preparing for yourself by introducing into your heart and soul the vibrations, the energy and life of the sun. It is by means of exercises of this kind that you will one day identify with the Deity.

The fact that we have this ability to identify with other beings or things means that in reality we are more than we appear. As individuals we are X, Y or Z, with a particular physical appearance, an identity, a name and so on. But in our soul and spirit we are far more than that. We are the whole universe; we are all beings. Literature holds many examples of this kind of experience, but many people consider it madness – or at best, poetic imagination. For those who consider themselves "normal", someone who says that he exists in trees, lakes and mountains, in the stars and the sun, or that he senses that he is the Deity, is, of course, a poet or a madman. For certain religious institutions, indeed, he would be seen as a heretic who deserves to die. And yet, this poet, madman or heretic is only saying what every human being truly is.

What is more important for us than to know what we truly are? And we can know this only by identifying with the Godhead. The great spiritual Masters of India have summed up this work of identification in the phrase: "I am That". The same thought is echoed in Jesus' words: *The Father and I are one,*[1] and Jesus wants us to achieve the same identification that he achieved, for he tells us: *Be perfect as your heavenly Father is perfect.*[2]

Yes, but when human beings learn that God is their Father, instead of reflecting and looking into themselves to find signs of that divine heredity, they limit themselves to a superficial, childish interpretation of Jesus' words. God is their father? Why, that is amazing! If you have a father who is all-powerful and overflowing with love you can ask him anything. So they behave like spoiled, capricious, demanding children, convinced as they are that God will always be understanding and indulgent, whatever they do. They think they only have to say, "Dear God, I committed this or that sin, but I believe in you. Forgive me, for I know that you are kind and merciful," for God to enfold them in his embrace. No, that is not how it is! A few words and pious sentiments are not enough. God will send them away, telling them to clean themselves up first. God cannot embrace someone who comes before him with his face covered in dust or mud. However much a mother loves her child,

1 Jn. 10, 30.   2 Mt. 5, 48.

if he runs to hug her with a face smeared with jam or chocolate, she will tell him to go and wash himself first.

Well, God does the same. However great his love, he cannot embrace you unless you wash yourself, at least a little. What does this mean? It means that two substances of different natures cannot be fused into one, and since God is light, you cannot become one with him, you cannot identify with him unless you too become light. If you continue to be covered in dust and mud, you will continue to be external to God, you will have no bond with him.

A great many Christians continue to be children, babies. They think that since God is their Father he will welcome them however muddy and disheveled they are. Others, anxious to show how sublime a notion they have of God and how deeply they have meditated on the imperfections of human nature, claim that it is humility that makes them ignore this primordial aspect of Jesus' teaching, the identification with God. This is why I say, once again, that above all they are lazy. It is easier to emphasize all the imperfections that put an infinite distance between God and man than it is to begin working seriously.

All is in God, and God is in all, but it is in man that the consciousness of this presence begins. You will ask, "In that case, why do we

not have a more vivid consciousness of this?"
That can only be explained by analogy. When
God wishes to enter and manifest in a human
beings, it is as though he were amusing himself
by shining his consciousness through opaque
glass. And the opacity of this material is such
that he can no longer see himself. He is, as it
were, obliterated, lost within us. For the divine
consciousness to awaken in our soul, our matter
has to become transparent. Only when this is so
can God say: "At last I recognize myself. This is
I. I am here." And in the same instant, we too
sense his presence.

It is because our consciousness is darkened
that God does not recognize himself. But as he
never ceases working on us and in us, if we
associate ourselves with his work, in the long
run he will recognize himself in us. Since it
was he who created us, it is from him that we
have received our ability to reflect and
understand. It is with these faculties that we
explore the external world as well as our own
inner world, and gradually, as we refine these
faculties, we become more conscious of our
divine identity.

Of course, I will not deny that certain
revelations can be dangerous. Not everyone is
ready to understand Jesus' words: *Be perfect as
your heavenly Father is perfect*, or, *You are
gods*, or again, *He who believes in me, the works*

*that I do he will do also; and greater works than
these will he do.*[3] But these revelations are there.
They have been written down, copied and
printed for centuries, and the task of the Church
was to explain them and thus prepare human
beings to understand them. But there are priests
who would say, "What if people should fall into
the sin of pride?" Well, it is very charitable of
them to want to preserve human beings from
pride –as though they had not found many other
ways of becoming proud! When human beings
no longer know what principles to base their
faith on, they end by saying that they have no
need of God, and declaring themselves unbelievers or atheists. What would you call that?
Humility or pride?

Humankind is now sufficiently evolved on
the psychic and intellectual levels to be given
access to these spiritual truths. Naturally, one
must be prudent, but then prudence is needed in
every area of life. It must not be used as an
excuse to continue concealing from human
beings the truth of their origins. This is something they need to know. It is because they do
not know who they are that they also have no
idea why they are on earth – unless it is to get
the maximum advantage from all the material
amenities produced by scientific and techno-

3 Jn 14, 12.

logical progress, even if, in order to do so, they have to fight tooth and nail and ruin or even destroy their neighbor.

Salvation lies in our ability to recognize our divine filiation. But in order for the Deity to manifest in you, you have to strive, more and more, to identify with him, while at the same time taking certain precautions. In the first place, when you are conscious that God dwells in you, you must also be conscious that he dwells equally in all human beings. In this way you will always be humble, unpretentious, friendly, comprehensive and open to others. The world does not need so-called divinities who only know how to order people about and impose their will... who are incapable of respect for their neighbor. Such people are a public menace! Not to mention the risks they themselves run of becoming unbalanced, even insane.

Secondly, in doing this exercise of identi-fication with God, be careful not to start thinking that you are God himself. That really is pride, and pride makes us opaque; it cuts us off from God. Simply try to feel that it is not you who exist, that only God exists, and that he exists in you only to the extent to which your unceasing work makes it possible for him to manifest.

But you must not delude yourself. Even if

you manage to create the higher state of
consciousness in which you become one with
God, you must realize that you cannot be
permanently in that state. It is not possible. It
may become possible later, perhaps in a few
thousand years, but in the meantime your
consciousness necessarily has its ups and
downs, and this is no reason to be discouraged.
Even a very brief experience of this kind will
reflect on your everyday behavior. And when
you have to return to more prosaic activities – as
you inevitably will – your state of consciousness
while carrying out these tasks will be
completely different.

It is important that this question be very
clear for you. Every effort, every exercise of a
spiritual nature produces results, but you must
not imagine that because you have been able to
melt into cosmic consciousness for a few
seconds, your thoughts, feelings and acts will
always be inspired by your divine nature.
Unfortunately not! Your lower nature will
continue to have its say, and you must try to be
even more lucid and watchful than before. For
there is nothing more detrimental to the spiritual
life than a lack of lucidity about oneself. It is not
terribly serious to make a mistake, on the
condition that you are aware of it. What is really
serious is to believe that you are inspired by the
Spirit when in fact you are following the

dictates of your grossest instincts.

Identification with God does not consist in convincing yourself that you have succeeded in climbing to his level and that from that height you can proclaim yourself to be omniscient and all-powerful. When you practice this exercise, tell yourself instead that you are allowing God's immensity to fill your being, and that you efface yourself before that immensity. It is by effacing oneself that one grows and becomes more resolute. The law of polarization is operative in this area as in others: greatness and smallness attract each other. God, who is infinitely great, loves what is infinitely small. If you become small, God will draw you to him. It is humility that makes it possible to become one with him.

We find this idea expressed in the Sephirotic Tree. Those who are humble attract the gifts of Chesed, the Sephirah of forgiveness and mercy, which is ruled by Jupiter. Whereas the proud arouse the powers of the opposite Sephirah, Geburah, severity, whose task is to restore order wherever it is threatened. And order is threatened whenever a presumptuous being stands up before God and claims to be his equal. To identify with God does not mean that you have to go to the point of declaring yourself his equal. No, that would be to lose your mind. The truth is that the proud have a shell which separates them from God. They think that they are growing bigger, but in reality it is not they but a tumor that is swelling within them. To be blown up is not the same as to grow bigger. The true growth of a being causes him to radiate rays, sparks and vibrations for the benefit of all.

The human soul is a very old entity. It possesses great knowledge, but it needs a lot of time and must make great efforts for this knowledge to rise to the surface. So many layers of opaque matter lie between us and our divine consciousness. This is why there is only one thing for us to do: apply the methods that enable us to break up the slag and deposits of waste within us which are an obstacle to the manifestation of divine wisdom, power and love.

Alchemists of old searched for the universal solvent. Why? Because they sought to dissolve all that opaque matter in them, that evil influence, that dangerous guide, which inhibits the union with God. This solvent is humility. And humility is effective if one knows *why* one should be humble. Even here, therefore, a certain amount of preliminary knowledge is necessary, for it is not a question of depreciating or disparaging oneself without discernment. If humility is not properly understood it can do as much damage as pride. True humility is that which enables us to dissolve our lower nature so that we may identify with the Deity.

11

GOD IS LIFE

In all religions, the supreme God is seen as the unique source of life. It is he who gives life, he who withdraws it. He is the Master of life, because he is life. What do we know about life? We can do no more than enumerate its many manifestations and say that in it all things are possible, that it contains all gifts – but it is still a mystery. As for God, so for life: all our attempts to grasp its secrets are destined to fail. Biologists, playing at being sorcerer's apprentices, have some success with their tinkering, and this success may delude them for a moment into thinking that they have grasped those secrets, but they are soon obliged to acknowledge their failure, for life belongs to God alone. God gives life, but he does not give the secret of creation, for it is his alone: he is life.

Like all creatures in the universe, human beings are depositories of life, but only depositories. Their superiority over other earthly creatures lies in their ability to receive this life not only through the physical body, but also through their heart and mind, their soul and spirit. And for this life to manifest fully, they have to be consciously linked to its Source, God.

Because the existence of human beings is a succession of efforts, suffering and obstacles to be overcome, they are obliged to struggle, and struggles exhaust their energies and leave them weaker. You can see this happening: day by day, something within them tarnishes and crumbles. Why? Because they do not know how to link themselves to the ever-flowing, inexhaustible Source, the only one that can give them ever-new waters, ever-new life. To be alive is to be capable of renewing and regenerating oneself. But those who truly know what it means to renew oneself are rare. Most people think that something that is different is necessarily new. No, change is not always a renewal. Only that which comes from the divine source is new, truly new, and it is to that source that we must be linked in order to regenerate ourselves.

It is so difficult to get human beings to understand the realities of the subtle worlds if they have not been prepared for them. This is why I will use another example taken from everyday life. Your house is equipped with electrical appliances which enable you to have heat and light. How do you do this? You plug them in. You plug in your lamp, and you have light. You plug in your heater, and you have warmth. You plug in your radio or television, and you receive a broadcast. The electricity installed in your house which makes it possible for your appliances to function comes from a power station. So if you do not plug in your lamp, your heater or your radio to that source, you will be in the dark, shivering with cold and unable to hear the messages broadcast around the world. Well, the power station symbolizes God, and all that makes life possible comes from that source. This means that by trying to do away with God, you are putting yourself in the worst possible conditions of darkness and spiritual cold... I can find no words to express the enormity of such blindness!

To be alive, both physically and spiritually, we need to be plugged in to the power station of life. Perhaps some of you will say, "All right, we understand that, but how do we plug in? We have no wires. No plugs." This is where you are mistaken. I have already explained that cosmic intelligence has endowed human beings with subtle centers which enable them to commun-icate with spiritual regions. These centers are the equivalent in the world of the soul and spirit of our physical sense organs, and the first step is to be conscious of them. At the same time we must adopt rules of conduct which make it possible to develop them. We are not asked to respect all these practices, all these rules given by the initiates – which we call the rules of morality – simply because we have to submit to passing human conventions, or in order to please a God who lives who-knows-where, up above the clouds. The true reason is that every one of our thoughts, feelings and acts has repercussions in the depths of our being and contributes either to enriching or to impoverishing the life within us.

God has given us life, but we have a good deal of work to do to be truly alive. It is up to us to reinforce the life that has been given to us; to make it more beautiful, subtler and more spiritual. There are many different levels of life. Those who remain on the lower levels can be in communication only with the realities of their level. They cut themselves off from the Source... and then they say, "Nothing has meaning. God does not exist." The reaction is normal. How could they perceive higher realities? When people remain on such a low level of consciousness, how can they rejoice in the existence of God? They cannot sense his presence either in themselves or around them. To sense the presence of divine life, you have to begin by making your own life divine. It is the divine life in us that awakens the spiritual centers which make it possible to sense the existence of God.

There is no need to ask whether God exists, therefore, before deciding on the orientation we want to give to our life. In fact, we should do the exact opposite: begin by endowing each moment of our life with ever-richer meaning. If we do this we will have no need to ask questions about the existence of God. It will have become self-evident. God is life, the fullness of life, and to sense his presence we need to become alive and to discover that everything around us is also alive. The earth is alive. Water is alive. Air, fire and light are alive. What can a corpse feel? Whatever you give it, it cannot react because life has left it. It can no longer feel anything. In order to feel you have to be alive. You will say that you know this... Yes, you know it theoretically. Every one knows it. But to know it is not enough; that is why we meet so many walking corpses.

There is a Being on whom we are totally dependent. That is why we have to maintain unbroken contact with him and have the courage to stand up to all inner or outer impulses to put obstacles in our way. Those who get rid of their faith in the first Cause can only profane and defile everything both in them-selves and all around them, for they cut themselves off from the source of life. Life comes from above; it is the quintessence of God himself, and this is why, in everything we do, we have a duty to welcome it, to open ourselves to it and learn to preserve it in all its light, all its wealth and power, so that we may be able to spread it all around us as well. We sometimes meet people who have this gift of receiving and disseminating, of radiating life wherever they go. You will usually find them among those who are very spiritual or among artists, but they can also be completely unassuming people with little schooling. Intellectuals, people of great learning, who are used to analyzing and dissecting everything, cut themselves off from life. This is why they are unhappy and dried up and are often so wrong: they do not possess the true intelligence of life.

Try to cultivate your consciousness of the divine life which penetrates all things, and you will sense many subtle, luminous beings around you. Some religions call these beings angels. Angels are emanations of the divine life – cabbalistic tradition teaches that they are bearers of pure life – and they manifest every time you manage to experience a moment of great spiritual intensity. Certain mystical emotions, certain qualities of silence, certain vibrations in the atmosphere of a room in which you have just been praying and meditating... all these are manifestations of an angelic presence.

You say that you cannot see them. True, but then you cannot see your thoughts or feelings either – or even your life, for that matter – but that does not mean that you doubt their existence. Their manifestations are proof enough. What we see is never more than the shell, the outward appearance of things. The essence is always hidden. So you may not see the angels, but you will sense their presence, and that presence is a sensation which you cannot doubt. That is life: the vibrations and currents flowing throughout space.

All life is dependent on God, the cosmic Source. It is because of it that birds sing, flowers bloom, the sun and the stars shine. The Source sustains and nourishes all beings. You must make a note of this idea not only in your notebooks but on the pages of your inner book. The Cabbalists say: "Inscribe the name of God on your door, on your roof, on your body, on your face and hands, in your soul... everywhere." Because we are alive only if we are capable of maintaining the link with God.

When I was a young disciple of the master Peter Deunov in Bulgaria, I noticed a habit of his which intrigued me. One suddenly had the impression that he would forget everything around him and go deep into himself, and then with an almost imperceptible movement of the lips he would say a few words which were impossible to distinguish. This could happen at any time. Whatever he was doing, there would always come a moment when he would stop and close his eyes and utter these few words, and, as though he had withdrawn into another world, his face expressed something extraordinarily peaceful and profound.

Naturally, I never dared to question him about this, but one day I managed to distinguish the words: *Slava na tebe, Gospodi!*, meaning "Glory to you O Lord", and I said to myself, "If even a great Master, who is always closely linked to God needs to say his name several times a day, how much more should we do so!" I wanted to imitate him. And now, in the course of the day, wherever I may be, I have the habit of repeating: *Slava na tebe, Gospodi!* And you can do the same, in Bulgarian or English, as you please. It takes only a few seconds. At home, at work or in the street, pause for an instant to make contact with the Creator and say these words silently to yourself, and you will immediately feel yourself linked to the divine Source of life.

But I repeat and insist: what is essential is the consciousness you put into simple exercises of this kind. Even if they take no more than a few seconds, do them with the sense that you are doing something sacred. It is the intensity that counts, not the time it takes. Have you never felt suddenly and inexplicably happy when a thought or feeling has flitted through you, completely changing your inner landscape? It is as though the rest of the day were illuminated. And how much more powerful must be the thought of God, of the Source who distributes the fullness of life! But it all depends on the importance you attach to that thought. To begin with, try to repeat this formula once an hour... Glory to you O Lord! And after a while, quite spontaneously, the need to do so will become like the need to breathe.

It is our task to glorify God on earth just as the angels glorify him in heaven. Of all the thousands of talks the Master gave, one in particular made such an impression on me that it is always the first to come to mind. We were on one of the peaks of the Rila massif, and the Master was talking about the work we have to do to glorify God. This was several decades ago, and I can no longer recall the exact words he used, but they were so luminous that, for me, they were a revelation; they put their seal on me for the rest of my life. My most vivid memory is of my feelings when I heard the Master saying that nothing was more important than to dedicate ourselves to glorifying God by our words, looks, gestures and everything we do, for this is how we make contact with the Source of life.

"To give glory..." What does the word

"glory" mean for most people? They are too dazzled by human glory to understand what the glory of God represents. In sacred art, paintings and sculptures, Christ or the triad of the Holy Trinity is always depicted surrounded by rays of light, and it is these rays of light that we call a "glory" or aureole. So glory is the luminous, brilliant manifestation of the divine life.

God is not one of those vain and tyrannical monarchs who demand to be acclaimed for their wealth, their virtues and their exploits, and who need to overshadow everyone else. God does not even need us to vaunt his merits. Our words are so poor that nothing we say can add anything to his glory. But it is we who need to glorify God so that we may be imbued with his glory. To glorify God means more than repeating how great, powerful and holy he is. That is not enough. We glorify him by bonding with him, by working to purify our thoughts and feelings, our desires and actions. This is how we become imbued with the light of divine glory, and wherever that light falls, we will be there.

12

GOD IN CREATION

The first article of faith for most believers is that God is the creator of heaven and earth. They repeat this in their prayers... they even sing it. Now, if God is the creator of heaven and earth, he must be present in the whole of creation, in every atom of creation, even in stone. Yes, even stone is an aspect of God, a manifestation of God. God is in light and he is also in stone. What a distance between stone and light, and yet the divine presence is active in both. In these few words you have all the wisdom of the initiates. Such a simple truth, and yet so far from human comprehension! It takes only a few seconds to state it, but it takes years to explain it, and it will take centuries, millennia, before we can all realize it.

Everything that exists in the universe participates in the same divine quintessence. How could God not put something of his own life into every particle of the universe he created? Polytheism, in fact – which Christians have so fiercely contested – is simply one way of saying that the whole of nature is inhabited by God. You must not think that the Hindu, Egyptian and Greek Pantheons were the product of naïve and superstitious human minds. Even Judaism – which was the first religion in history to insist on the reality of one God – yes, even in Judaism the Cabbalah speaks of God under different names which express his different attributes and manifestations in the universe.

Now, picture someone who knows nothing about Christianity going into a church: what would he see? People kneeling in front of the image of a man nailed to a cross, who they say is the only son of God. Or they will be praying before a bird, a dove, which they call the Holy Spirit and which represents the third person of a family they call the Holy Trinity. He would also see quantities of paintings or statues representing angels, archangels, the Virgin Mary and the saints, and in front of them would be the faithful, lighting candles and praying to them for health, success, the love of their life, the disappearance of their enemies and so on. In your opinion, what would that person think? Would he not think that Christians too – even though they preach the reality of one God – actually address their prayers to all kinds of divinities?

You will say, "Yes, but the difference between monotheism and the polytheistic religions is that we do not worship the forces of nature, the stars or the four elements; also, animals and plants are not considered sacred." That is true, but do you think that objects such as statues, paintings or stained-glass windows, all made by human hands, are better inter-mediaries between you and the Godhead than the things of nature which God has filled with his own life? It is time for Christians to expand their consciousness a little and understand that all religions – through many forms, some elaborate and some less so – express the same ideas: that God, who created the universe, reveals himself through all the living mani-festations of that universe of which we still know only an infinitesimal part.

If you want to know the universe, it is not enough to study it with the help of the instruments that are now available. We must also interact with it. This interaction, this give and take, already occurs naturally, for we cannot survive without some exchange with the world around us. Beginning with the need to breathe and eat, our life is made up of countless forms of exchange. Our organs and the senses of touch, taste, smell, hearing and sight have also been given to us for the purpose of exchange. Our intellectual and emotional life is also made up of encounter and exchange. Through speech, feelings and thoughts we are constantly weaving the network of communications which is the basis of family and social life. But for most human beings, this interaction is still on an unconscious, instinctive level – and this means that there is not much to distinguish them from animals and plants. Plants and animals also breathe and nourish themselves. Animals are also endowed with sense organs – in fact, in many animals, the sense of smell, hearing and sight are more highly developed than in human beings. They also have a familial and social life which is often a source of astonishment to the observer.

So, what must we human beings do? We must become aware that these different forms of exchange which we need for survival are made possible for us thanks to powers and entities with which the Creator has peopled the universe and which are different manifestations of his presence. Even if we cannot see them, those entities are there to help us to find nourishment through the air, through the light of the sun and through all living beings. It is thanks to the sacrifice of these entities, thanks to their love and their desire for exchange with us that we are still alive, still physically, psychically and spiritually alive. So we must learn to be in communication with them, to regard them with respect, as precious beings who have to be approached carefully, with delicacy and musicality... Yes, musicality.

It depends entirely on us to sense the divine presence in every instant of our everyday life. Even when we are eating, God is there. Since food contributes life, God must be present in food, and we should regard nutrition as a sacred act. Of course, some theologians will claim that we should see God only in the bread and wine of Communion. But if he were not truly present also in our ordinary food, it would mean that there are places from which he is absent. In reality God is omnipresent. He is present everywhere in the form of life. If life existed apart from him, it would mean that some other being had put it there... And who could that be?

To have a sense of all the wealth and beauty of life, you need to seek the presence of God everywhere. If you do this, each day will bring new discoveries, and above all, you will become stronger. There is no more effective way to confront difficulties than to augment and intensify life in oneself. But what do most human beings do? They spend their time racing to the periphery of life in search of what they call success, accomplishment and happiness – and for them, happiness is often synonymous with ease. But the ease they seek can so readily be destabilized by events, and when this happens, their whole life collapses. You need to find the firm, unwavering point within that nothing can disturb. Even if you suffer, even if you lose everything you have, you still sense the presence of something steadfast and unshakable within, something which survives all tribulations. This is what it means to have faith.

To have faith is to sense the reality of the divine world through all that we experience in our daily lives. For faith, too, needs nourishment. It is nourished by our awareness of the riches with which God has endowed everything around us – the earth, water, air, light – and it is nourished by our efforts to work with them. What is the use of repeating that we believe in God, creator of heaven and earth, if we never do anything to allow heaven and earth to strengthen our faith in him? We are unconscious, inattentive and superficial. We sever our link with the source of life, and then we say: "Nothing has any meaning. There is no God." The truth is that if you did nothing more than learn to nourish yourself consciously, to breathe consciously, you would perceive that meaning and sense the presence of God. After certain experiences you will necessarily sense the presence in you and around you of that sublime Being who created all things.

Life is immense, full of meaning and riches which are still hidden to human beings, and this is why even believers have difficulty in basing their faith on solid foundations. Yes, even they are incapable of a relationship of exchange because they are closed in on themselves. They are, of course, obliged to relate to a few people and to nature itself, but those relationships remain superficial, for they have never learned that, through them, they could be in touch with divine life. They are shut up in the depths of their own being like prisoners in a cell, with no light and barely enough food to keep them alive. They feel alone and cut off from everything. But this feeling of solitude is an illusion. If human beings were less walled-in, less self-centered, they would become conscious of the reality of an invisible world whose inhabitants are there beside them, mingling with them, for through their thoughts and feelings they attract these creatures.

Whether we are alone in the midst of nature or in our own room, in reality we are never alone; these entities share in every moment of our lives. Those who work for good are accompanied by luminous entities which rejoice with them and help them in their difficulties, by showing them solutions and ways out of their problems. Most of the time this happens without their realizing it. But if they make an effort to be aware of these presences they will, of course, benefit even more from them.

The Creator has given human beings everything. He has put everything at their disposition, but they persist in leading such superficial lives that they get almost no benefit from his gifts. You only have to look at the relationship most people have with nature, animals, trees or flowers...

Take flowers, for instance. Is there anyone who does not love flowers? We all like to give or receive them; we put them in our houses and plant them in our gardens. We go and admire them in parks or in the country and are enchanted by their forms, colors and scents, but we consider them primarily as decorative elements which contribute to making life more agreeable. So even our admiration is superficial, and we gain very little from the presence of all these flowers. In actual fact, flowers are living beings with whom it is possible to relate. Yes, a flower is not simply a morsel of colored, scented matter, it is the home of a spiritual entity who has come to talk to us of heaven and earth. If we know how to look at a flower, how to bond with it, through it we can relate to the forces of nature, to all those subtle creatures that work to make it such a vivifying and poetic presence.

Take the example of the rose, which has had such an important place in the history of religions, art and literature, even in the life of certain societies. Roses are everywhere, people constantly make gifts of them, but what good does this really do? Once they have been put in a vase no one pays them any attention. And yet a rose becomes more alive if you look at it with an enlightened awareness, and a relationship is established between you and it. You sense the splendid being who is dwelling in that flower and speaking to you. Some of you may say, "That's not possible. It's only for fairy-tales... We can't possibly hear flowers talking!" Ah, but there are different ways of hearing the voice of a flower, and if what I say seems to be drawn from a fairy-tale, you must not forget that fairy-tales are not just pretty stories invented for children by people with a lot of imagination. They correspond to a very profound reality that you will be able to grasp only when you manage to open yourself to a relationship of exchange with the whole of nature.

Suppose you have a tree in your garden: you can see it for years without paying attention, as though it were part of a theatrical backdrop made of cardboard or plaster. But you can also become aware of it as a living being. You can even approach it to greet it and talk to it and become imbued with what it represents. For a tree is a magnificent and extraordinarily profound symbol. You will say, "What difference does that make?" Of course, physically, materially, it makes no difference. But on the etheric level the tree will be enriched by your life and you by its life. In fact, it is you who stand to gain the most. The day human beings decide to pay attention to the mysteries of life instead of burdening themselves with all kinds of useless things, they will make some fantastic discoveries.

Already, when I was very young, I began to experience the things I have been talking about... and I continue to do so today. I talk to the trees in my garden and to those in the forest, when I walk there. I caress and even hug them. Why? Because I sense that they are alive, and I want to communicate with that life which flows from the roots to the tips of the branches. And then I communicate with the invisible creatures that dwell in the trees and look after them. For just as there are entities that look after human beings, there are also those that look after stones, plants and animals.

An excursion in the woods will always be beneficial. As you walk and breathe the pure air, you will feel more peaceful. But you can do far more than that. Perhaps you find it difficult to believe that human beings can communicate with trees. Well, you are free not to believe, but this only shows that you have not studied the question properly. If you had, you would now know and be able to communicate with the soul of all trees. To say, "I don't believe," simply means, "I haven't studied. I am ignorant."

It all depends on how you consider people and things. If your consciousness is enlightened, your thoughts can be the starting point of magnificent realizations. But without that consciousness, you will reject the riches that are offered; you will understand nothing, gain nothing. We only need to see how human beings live side by side: they meet and pass each other with no more consciousness of their mutual presence than if they were blocks of wood. Look at how they jostle and bump into each other... To expect them to sense the life of nature is asking too much of them. They need to change something in their consciousness. They claim to be the only beings who are truly alive and intelligent, and to prove how alive and intelligent they are, they limit themselves, shut out the light and kill off everything within them. There you have the truth, the sad truth.

We are in the universe as in a sanctuary which we should approach with the awareness that it is sacred. For nature is alive, and not only alive, it is also intelligent. If we open ourselves to it, it responds by allowing us to participate in its life. Some may say, "But natural phenomena happen mechanically. There is no intelligence involved." Yes, human beings have seen that the universe obeys laws, and this has made it possible for them to create what they call "the

natural sciences", but that is no reason to
conclude that natural phenomena are purely
mechanical. If you envisage things that way, you
will be depriving yourself of life; you will be
making it impossible for life to pour itself into
your heart, into your soul, into your mind, even
into your physical body. You will become truly
alive only when you make up your minds to
enter into a relationship with the life that is
present throughout the universe.

And to start with, there is the earth with all
its treasures, all its wonders – the earth which
makes seeds germinate, which nourishes the
roots of all plants. How can anyone fail to
believe that the earth, too, is alive? Yes, alive
and intelligent! Have you never thought about
the earth's ability to transform all the carcasses
and rotting remains of the human, animal and
vegetable kingdoms? It accepts filth that would
make you turn away in disgust and transforms
it, giving us in its stead magnificent trees and
flowers, cereal crops, vegetables and succulent
fruits. What extraordinary alchemical laboratories does it have at its disposal? So why not
go to the earth and ask it to help you in your
own work of transformation. Sit on the ground,
make a small hole in the soil and put a finger in
it, while saying: "O earth, my mother, you have
given me my body and you nourish me every
day... I have a request to make: since you have

the power to transform even the foulest matter, I ask you to take my impurities and all that is dirty in me and to transform them and give them back to me in the form of matter as pure as crystal..."

And when you wash your hands... What is more ordinary than to wash one's hands? And yet in reality nothing is ordinary, nothing is insignificant if you do it consciously. The water you are touching is the material expression of the invisible water that flows through the universe. By washing your hands consciously you can be in touch with that cosmic water; you can ask it to purify you, but you can also confide your thoughts and feelings, all your most intimate desires for your own good and that of the whole world.

Some may be appalled by this: "If you advise us to pray to the earth and water you are asking us to behave like pagans!" To that I can only say it is no more pagan than to pray in front of a statue or a painting of a saint. If you protest at the idea, it shows that you have not even begun to understand what you are doing when you pray. Suppose you have an icon or a holy picture at home: morning and evening you light a candle and ask it to protect you. But what do you really believe? It is not the icon that will protect you. The icon is nothing more than an object of wood or cardboard. What will protect you is the state induced within you by your prayer and meditation, the imprints of which will remain in you and guide you in the way of light, love and peace.

You are the only one who can really do anything for yourself. A picture can only be a starting point, a prop. Of course, it is possible for the icon in front of which you have prayed every day for years and years to become something truly alive and powerful, but if it does, it is thanks to you, thanks to the life you have put into it. Of itself it can give you nothing. Similarly, if you speak to the earth or to water, it is not because you think they are all-powerful deities who can answer your prayers, but because they are props for your inner work. And as props, they are all the more effective in that they are alive, alive with the life of God himself. The same is true of air and of fire.

You can nourish your inner life only by becoming conscious of all the living beings around you. So when you are in the midst of nature, remember to speak to its inhabitants, as well as to the angels of the four elements. Say, "Blessings on you, angels of earth, water, air and fire. Blessings on you, O faithful servants of God! And you, children of nature, spirits who inhabit caves and forests, mountains, seas, lakes and rivers; all you who dwell in the wind, the clouds, the sun... blessings on you!" From all sides, a multitude of entities will draw near and crowd around you to listen to you, telling themselves that here, at last, is someone who recognizes that they exist and who blesses them. They are happy, they sing and dance, and you, in return, receive something that will make you stronger and more alive.

Speaking of Christ, St Paul says: *In him we live and move and have our being.*[1] If even Christians have no sense of that reality, it is simply because they do not open themselves. Immersed in water, they are still thirsty. Immersed in God, they forget him; they do not see, do not sense that he is giving them life. They are closed. If only they would make a tiny opening in the depth of their being, the divine ocean would pour into them and flood them with its blessings. But as long as they fail to be open, as long as they fail to comprehend the power of exchange, they will remain parched, poor and alone.

To make exchanges with life means to pause before even the slightest manifestation of the lives that surround us, to look at them, listen to them, respect and love them. For this world that is all around us is also within us. Rivers, mountains, the sun, the stars... we have ties with the whole of nature, ties that we need to

1 Acts, 17, 28.

intensify. The purpose of life is, quite simply, to live, and we can live only by weaving ties with all the living beings that people that universe: nature spirits, but also the angels, archangels and divinities, all the way to the Creator himself, to him who put his own life into each being and each thing. This is how faith should be taught to children.

All that is in us and around us speaks to us of the presence of God. But what is extraordinary is that this is not enough for human beings. They want God to show himself to them in person. The truth is, that for many, even this would not be enough. They would find a way to see nothing, hear nothing, feel nothing. God would have to come to them with thunder and lightning to break through their armor, and this is something he will not do. He leaves human beings to find the means to discover him within themselves.

You will say, "Yes, but if God were more visibly present it would help us." Do you really believe that? Think of this: what is more present, more visible, more luminous than the sun? But if you always take refuge behind closed shutters, you will not even be aware that it exists. If you want to see it, you will have to open at least one window, because the sun is not going to force its presence on you by breaking through your walls and shutters. In the same way, if you want to discover the presence of God, you must open at least one small fanlight. Yes, it is you, it is we, who have to do something, not God. God does what he has to. He is there; that should be enough for us. It is up to us to do whatever is necessary to sense his presence. A higher level of consciousness exists, and it never ceases to reveal the meaning and beauty of the world to us; how can we fail to be aware of that presence? For this is God. God within us. And we discover him progressively by becoming gradually more aware that life is rich and full of meaning.

Of course, I do not deny that God is totally inconceivable to human beings, but as his kindness and generosity make him want to reveal himself to them, his creation is full of all kinds of signs he has placed there to enable us to find him. The trouble is that human beings do not try to find these signs, and even when they have them before their eyes, they do not decipher them. The result is that the Deity in whom they believe remains an abstraction for them. And as they cannot live on abstractions, they have manufactured more and more statues, medals, crosses and holy pictures, so many concrete, material representations of God that it often becomes infantile and ridiculous.

If Christianity supposedly represented a step forward in the spiritual history of humanity, at the moment, because of Christians themselves, this is not very visible. If you tell Christians to attend the sunrise in the morning, they will be scandalized; they will have the impression that you are telling them to revert to paganism. Not only does a Christian not find God in the universe he created, but above all, he will not seek him in the sun, the source of life. He prefers to seek him in churches built by human hands, in the midst of statues and pictures manufactured by humans... As you can see, that is much better!

Life is the power of powers. Only the sun can give us some idea of this reality. In it we see two manifestations of life: light and heat. And as I have told you time and again, if Christians were willing to open themselves to the sun, they would understand better what they call the mystery of the Holy Trinity, the mystery of one God in three persons, Father, Son and Holy Spirit. The Father represents the life from which proceed the Son and the Holy Spirit, light and heat, wisdom and love. But what can I do if Christians refuse to understand that only the sun can corroborate this, the very foundation of their religion, and make it comprehensible to them? What can I do if, when I talk to them about meditating at sunrise, they think I want to turn them back to the ancient cults which saw the sun as a god to be adored?

It was the Master Peter Deunov, in Bulgaria, who established the practice of attending the sunrise in spring and summer. There are so many things you can understand when watching the sun rising, so many exercises you can do to be impregnated by this life, light and warmth. Already, at first light, the heavens are preparing for a great event... all those clouds, dark or light, appearing and disappearing... all the colors of the dawn sky, like so many presences heralding the dazzling manifestation of the sun! But how many people are aware of what the birth of each new day represents? How many see in this tireless repetition that has been going on for billions of years a reenactment of the birth of the first morning of the world? Think of all the beings, visible and invisible, who are present at this prodigious dawning of light...

Human beings are so unaccustomed to using their God-given psychic and spiritual faculties that they have no idea what to do when they see the sun rising. They soon start yawning with boredom. They are tired of watching that brilliant sphere in the sky. So they leave the sun and go to take care of more tangible, more important things... What is so extraordinary is that many people, finding themselves by chance in front of the rising sun, acknowledge that it is one of the most beautiful sights one can see, but that does not mean they are ready to make an effort to renew the experience. Yes, how many would feel impelled to get up early to greet the dawn, to welcome that light into their hearts and souls so that the whole day may be luminous and pure?

The sun is the most perfect image of God. But in spite of that perfection, it is still only a form, and you must go further to seek God beyond that form. God must always be sought above and beyond forms. So, when you are gazing at the sun, try to sense that you are gazing at God's most perfect representative on earth. This sensation will contribute to raising the vibrations of your being to a higher level. All the elements will be exalted in you; you will be launched into the farthest regions of space, and even the notion of time will be abolished. Like God, you will be living in eternity. And now, know that what I am telling you is true; there are entities here who are listening and broadcasting it to the whole world.

13

RABOTA, VREME, VERA
WORK, TIME, FAITH

In every domain, it is possible to find men and women who create masterpieces or carry out great exploits. You will say, "That is normal. They are very gifted." I agree, they are gifted, but even the most gifted person in the world cannot achieve anything if he does not practice, often from childhood, every day, several hours a day. Before someone can pour out such wealth, seemingly effortlessly, he must have already taken tremendous pains and overcome great difficulties.

Work... Work is the only way to get results, and this is even more true in the spiritual life than in any other domain. Why? Because the spiritual life cannot be separated from life in its totality. Take the case of a musician: even if he is a genius, even if he dedicates his life to music, music does not take up every corner of his life. He can cultivate his talent while still giving in to uncontrolled passions and leading a stupid, chaotic kind of life. The ability to excel in intellectual, artistic or physical activities has never protected anyone from the manifestations of his lower nature.

The truth is that it is easier to cultivate a talent, whatever it may be, than to tackle one's weaknesses and psychic defects, for this is the work of every moment, night and day. Yes, even at night it is possible to work on yourself if you know how to use the forces of the subconscious. But most human beings neglect this field of work and experience. In fact, I can tell you that if they devote themselves to artistic, intellectual and physical activities, it is more often than not because they are running away – running away from themselves. They unconsciously avoid looking at themselves so that they will not feel obliged to make an effort to improve. Yes, they run away, and in doing so they distance themselves from God. For the only way to find God is precisely this work of self-improvement. They do not distance themselves because they deliberately decide to reject God, but because they focus all their attention on activities in which they spread themselves too thin, and they end by losing themselves.

When I was a young disciple of the Master Peter Deunov, in Bulgaria, he would sometimes give me an interview, and as I was leaving, he would say: *Rabota, rabota, rabota, Vreme,*

vreme, vreme, Vera, vera, vera... Rabota means
work; *Vreme* means time, and *Vera* means faith.
He never explained why he said these three
words or what significance they had for him. At
first I was too young to understand, but I
thought about them a lot and as the years went
by I understood that all realizations – and in
particular all spiritual realizations – rest on
three factors: work, time and faith. This is why,
when people complain that, in spite of all the
efforts they make, they see no results, I can only
tell them, "That is for one of two reasons: either
you have not been working enough, or you do
not know how you should be working."

The spiritual life is ruled by the same laws as
the life of society. Take the case of someone
who has never done much work and who earns
very little. One day he needs a large sum of
money, because, for example, he needs to buy a
house to live in. If he goes and asks for it at the
bank, convinced that, since a bank has a lot of
money it will surely give him what he needs,
what kind of reception do you think he will get?
We all know that on the physical plane such a
request is bound to be disappointed, and yet on
the spiritual plane many people think their
application will be granted. They apply to
heavenly banks and clamor for miracles,
expecting angels and archangels to come and
help them. But what have they ever done to

deserve this? Is it enough to recite a few prayers in moments of difficulty for heaven to open its doors, the sun to stand still and the whole of nature to change its laws? If you have never done anything to deserve help from heaven, you will not get it.

Heaven is there, wide open, ready to pour out its blessings, but in order to receive them we must have prepared ourselves in advance by love and selflessness, patience and fidelity... All these virtues are fruits that we produce in order to give them to God. And if we do this, then yes, the day we ask for something, our prayer will be heard. Like those who have already accumulated some capital, we can ask to be paid something, if only the interest on it. Perhaps you will say, "That's not a very poetic analogy... and besides, money deposited in banks has not always been honestly come by." Oh, I know it only too well! But at least the analogy is clear. If you were all capable of understanding the truths of the spiritual life – which is true poetry – I would not have to use examples of this kind.

Many people acknowledge that if you want to be successful on the material plane, you have to be convinced and work without trying to cut corners, and yet they still imagine that the things you want on the spiritual plane can be obtained quickly and effortlessly. How wrong they are! You have to begin by working without relaxing your efforts. Secondly, you must not be in a hurry, because it always takes a long time to achieve something great. You must not try to rush things. Finally, you must really believe that your efforts will one day produce results, for nature is true and faithful, and the laws which govern it are never found wanting.

"Work, time, faith." You cannot begin to imagine the wealth contained in these three words. You can, of course, change the order and say "faith, work, time". But what really matters is to understand that these three factors are linked, and how they are linked. So there is only one thing for us to do: set to work with conviction without worrying about how long it will take to achieve our divine ideal. We have the keys; we have the powers; we have the means to remedy everything... but not all at once.

All those inner voices which encourage you to get up and start walking toward the light represent the capital earned by the work you did in the past. Yes, the urge we feel to move forward on the path of perfection is a result of efforts we have made in the past. And what happens when we make progress, however slight, on the spiritual plane? Forces that have been dormant within us for thousands of years are awakened and respond to our call. In this way, all of a sudden, we see that we are inhabited by a veritable army which is only waiting to be called to action. Every time we win a victory we discover the presence of unsuspected forces within us.

Sometimes, when you are required to make a great effort, you wonder if you are going to be able to do it. You hesitate a little, then you make up your mind, and presto! you lift the weight or remove the obstacle from your path. To see proof of what you are capable of makes you more aware of your powers, and when you sense your strength, your faith becomes stronger. Faith, therefore, is linked to the self-confidence born of success. Progressively, with each effort we make, our untried abilities are brought out into the light of day and begin to manifest. But we have to be realistic and begin humbly, with small things. So many people have arrested their own evolution because they failed to begin modestly.

Suppose you want to learn to play a musical instrument. If you try to master complicated pieces before spending long hours on preparatory exercises, you will soon give up, because the difficulties will be insurmountable. So you must begin by playing scales every day and spending a long time on exercises for beginners. If you want to go far you have to start off slowly and with great attention to detail. If you make a mistake when you first read a piece of music, that mistake will be recorded in your brain and you will be liable to repeat it every time. Look at an engraver tracing a design on a metal plate: he cannot allow himself to make a single error, for if he does, his tool will slip into the same groove every time and it will be impossible to correct it. To achieve something perfect, the first impression must be done slowly and carefully. The second time, you can do it a little faster; the third time faster still, and so on. And with psychic work, exactly the same rules apply. You must begin slowly, taking great care not to deviate, otherwise you will have to work very hard and make a tremendous effort to get back on the right track.

People think that by going fast they can save time, but in reality the opposite is true. This law has unimagined implications. In the inner life, a seemingly insignificant detail can have immense repercussions because of what it triggers in a person's consciousness. Someone whose endeavor meets with success senses his consciousness expanding, and it is this expansion that counts. But if his expectations are exaggerated, his endeavor will fail, and that failure will weaken something in him and will undermine his self-confidence. Human beings are capable of doing great things as long as they begin in a small way, and the greater the ambition, the more modest must be the first steps.

The greatest spiritual achievements depend on a few simple daily practices that I have often talked to you about: to learn to be calm, to eat in silence while concentrating on your food, to make contact with the four elements... and many more besides. So, do not begin by thinking, "Within a few months or a few years I will have overcome all my evil tendencies and will live in divine light." That is impossible, for you have been feeding those evil tendencies for many, many incarnations, and if you begin by deluding yourself in this way you will soon be discouraged.

What really matters is to become stronger, and for this you have to practice with very small things. What counts is not so much what you achieve but the fact that you are becoming stronger. To succeed in small things always strengthens your inner faith in great things, and if I tell you not to rush into major undertakings straight away, it is to help you avoid failures. But here, too, you have to understand: it is not the failure that matters, it is the fact that with each failure you lose a little of your faith, a little of your confidence. And if your faith and confidence diminish, the forces related to them also diminish. Perhaps you think I am talking about insignificant details. No! Little things are not necessarily insignificant. By underscoring them I want to arouse your attention, your curiosity, the desire to decipher them. If you reasoned about this more clearly, you would understand that my insistence means that these details are not insignificant, they are essential. Do you think me stupid enough to spend my life on things that are worthless? If they were so negligible, so useless, don't you think that I would have noticed it before now?

When you bring conviction to a physical effort, new energies build up in your muscles as well as in your nervous system, and you are more likely to succeed. But if you overestimate your strength and try to do something which is beyond your capacity, you will not succeed the first time, and doubt will begin to worm its way in and you will start to wonder if it is really worth trying again. This doubt paralyzes the forces that were available to you at your first attempt, so that you fail again. You fall into the chasm, figuratively speaking, that you were trying to jump over. Only faith and self-confidence are capable of triggering the extra influx of energy you need to bolster your efforts, so it is important not to wipe them out by beginning with something overly ambitious. There is plenty of time...

Heaven does not demand great exploits of you, it asks only that you never stop trying. Yes, heaven judges people by what they are capable of giving with the means at their disposal. You sometimes meet people who are truly deprived, people who were born into a family of paupers, who have been ill-treated and given the worst possible examples of behavior while they were growing up, who have bad health and little or no schooling, and yet who, by dint of continuous efforts and unwavering conviction, have managed to triumph over their circumstances and achieve things that others, more privileged, fail to achieve. Well, this is what heaven looks at when it sends us into the world: what we manage to do with the faculties we have received and the conditions in which we have lived. Life is so rich with possibilities that we can always find things to do to improve and enrich ourselves spiritually. This is what heaven most values in human beings: their ability to make the most of the slightest opportunity offered to them.

Very few people are capable of succeeding immediately in grandiose endeavors. There are fields such as sports, the arts, business and politics in which young people sometimes achieve spectacular success, but as that success very often lacks a solid foundation, their star usually sinks into obscurity as suddenly as it arose... and then how much suffering and how many lives wasted! It is true that there are exceptional beings who are never discouraged by failure; it stimulates them, in fact. But such beings are rare.

So, if you want to maintain a healthy psychological balance, you must begin in small things so as to gain courage from each new success. However, there is one psychological reality that you should know: if discouragement is bad, there is something that is worse, and that is stubbornness. Oh yes, one sees so many people obstinately determined to obtain or keep positions, functions, roles for which they are quite unfit. And they are proud of their stubbornness, for they want to show the world that nothing can stop them, nothing can force them to change or surrender. Well, it would be far better for people like that to be discouraged before their inflated ambitions bring about their fall and that of others.

It is excellent to have ambition, but ambitions that are not supported by the corresponding qualities can only end in catastrophe. Above all, you must never confuse ambition with a high ideal. What is the difference between the two? Ambition seeks visible, tangible, material success, whereas a high ideal seeks only spiritual, inner progress. Unfortunately, many spiritual people have never understood this difference. Some try to use spiritual means to obtain the power, money or glory they are incapable of achieving in their ordinary way of life through talent and hard work. Others, on the basis of some slight results on the spiritual plane, immediately imagine that they can represent themselves as Masters, capable of guiding souls. Here too, what mischief they can do to themselves and those around them!

Those who truly want to advance on the divine path try to remain in the shadows as long as possible. Not only do they not push themselves forward, but they are in no hurry to be pushed forward by others who claim to recognize them as spiritual guides. Before accepting such a function, one must be psychically very well armed and well protected, and this requires centuries of discipline and hard work. Those who are not properly prepared continually receive shocks, for others demand too much of them, and since they are not equipped to respond to those demands, they are constantly exposed to conflicts and accusations – even threats – and life becomes a nightmare.

Too few spiritualists are aware of the responsibilities they assume by daring to instruct and guide others through the labyrinth of their inner world. For at the heart of the labyrinth there is a monster waiting to devour them – you all know the story of the Minotaur. Only one who, for long years, has remained far from the limelight, studying and becoming stronger while cultivating the virtues of gentleness and humility, is in a position to guide others without the risk of misleading them or of being devoured by them.

Another difference – and one which is absolutely essential – between ambition and a high ideal is that those who are truly borne along by a high ideal are never disappointed. Unlike the failed ambitious, who are constantly mourning their lost illusions, the mere presence within spiritual people of a high ideal which nourishes and guides them is enough to make them happy. Yes. They know, they sense that they are on the right road, that nothing can prevent them from going forward, and this is enough... even though they occasionally stumble, for that is inevitable.

To have made up your mind to follow the right road is not a guarantee that you will never deviate. But here, too, you have to conserve your faith, and when you stumble or make some slight error, you must refuse to weep and wail and declare yourself "stupid, incompetent, weak and despicable..." That is merely a reaction of wounded pride. You must simply look the situation squarely in the face, and tell yourself: "That was just another manifestation of my lower nature, but I'm going to work at taming it. I'm going to put my wild animals in a cage. I have faith in the spirit within me. It is the spirit that will have the last word." Yes, that is what faith is: absolute confidence in the power of the spirit, the power of the indwelling God. So, even if you make mistakes, even if you stumble and fall, you must never stop. Get up and go on, in spite of your weaknesses, your falls, your faults and failings. Climb higher so as to be above your lower nature, and then you will see just what faith is capable of.

In the spiritual life, therefore, you must never worry about the time, but only about whether you are still moving forward on the path of light. As long as you are sure you are going toward the light, you must demand no conditions... just keep walking. Someone may say, "I'll be old before I get there!" So what? No need to worry about that either, otherwise you will do nothing... and still grow old! Yes, you are going to grow old in any case, but you will be old without light and without beauty. Well, believe me, it is better to be old with light, with beauty, with understanding, with love. Yes, that is well worth it. Heavens, what a strange view of life human beings have! How strangely they reason!

So, let this be quite clear: whatever you say or do, I will continue to tell you: *Rabota, rabota, rabota, Vreme, vreme, vreme, Vera, vera, vera...* I am like the master potter in the story... Ah, you don't know that story? It is a Bulgarian folk tale:

There was once a young boy who apprenticed himself to a master potter. His master told him, "You must work with me for three years and at the end of that time I will tell you the secret of how to make your pots very strong." The boy began to work. One year passed and then a second, and he thought he knew enough, so he left his master and began his own workshop. But all his pots broke, one after the other. Wondering about this, he said to himself, "There must be something I missed when I was with my master, or else he hid something from me. I'll go back to him." A little shamefaced, he presented himself to his master, who accepted him as his apprentice again, but on condition that he stay another three years. When the three years were up, his master said: "This is the secret: before you put your pots in the kiln you must blow on them." The apprentice was dumbfounded: "That's all?" he exclaimed; "You made me work for you for so many years for nothing but that?" "Yes," said the master potter; "That is all!"

Ah, but as this is a story, you must understand that to blow on the pots symbolized something...

Well, I too have a secret for making strong pots. Where are they, these strong pots? Here, of course, my pots are you... strong and durable because I have blown on you. You must not be insulted! When I say "pots" I mean, of course, distinguished vases, vases in which angels place flowers to be put before God. Yes, we are all vases. Our hearts, our souls are vases, choice vases fashioned by the divine Potter to contain the elixir of everlasting life. Is that not the most beautiful and most honorable future you could wish for? So you see, there is no need to feel insulted. Just work, work, work, to give these vases perfect shape, color and transparency.

Rabota, vreme, vera... Work, time, faith. Yes, especially *vreme*, time. This is why I so often say *"Bonne continuation"*, keep up the good work! To start a job is easy, but to persevere is difficult. Difficult, yes, but perseverance is what is essential. So, keep working, keep on... Someone ought to compose a song with this, something very tuneful... "Keep working..." and we would sing it together.

Even if you have a high ideal – especially if you have the very highest ideal – you must cultivate humility. It is humility that will keep you from imagining that, from one day to the next, you are going to be victorious in everything. Nothing is exempt from the law of work and, thus, from the law of time. The work before us is a work of hundreds, of thousands of years, and if we base our estimates on the span of a human life, we will always miscalculate. Ultimately, time is always the determining factor. It is always time that tells us whether or not we are on the right path, so we should not be in a hurry.

Those who are in a hurry inevitably meet with failure; then they become discouraged and stop trying, thus opening the door to evil.

The worst thing that can happen to us is to lose our taste for the work we need to do patiently, day after day, on ourselves. When this happens it means that we do not know the value of the treasures in our possession; we allow the gems God has placed in us – all those qualities and virtues – to lie un-mined and unused. Never, under any pretext, must this work be abandoned. We must never let up, but without worrying about visible results.

Just as precious stones always retain their value, the value of the qualities and virtues we bear within us can never be diminished. As long as we keep working on them, whatever comes, we need worry about nothing else. The slightest trace of doubt reveals our ignorance of this value. You want results, don't you? But actually, since you know that all that is good is eternal, have you not got them already? Perhaps you will say that all this is beyond you... Yes, I understand, but it does not matter. If you cannot grasp all this today, you will be able to do so later – in a year, ten years, twenty years, in another incarnation. What is certain is that you will understand them one day. When? When you have done your work. Don't you know that I, too, understand certain truths better each day.

Yes. Because I work.

Rabota, vreme, vera... Work, time, faith. Faith goes hand in hand with long-term work. It is the fruit of efforts repeated day after day. Faith is something that lives, something that we must never separate from our everyday life. This is what we need to understand if we are to discover the hidden meaning of Jesus' words: *if you have faith the size of a mustard seed, you will say to this mountain, "Move from here to there," and it will move.*[1]

We can move a mountain, but only if we do not rush at it, thinking to move it in one go. We can move a mountain, but only if we are ready to move it stone by stone. Every stone we move – that is, everything we succeed in doing, however small – increases our faith; we begin to feel that we are stronger and more stalwart, more in control of the situation. And then one day, if we look back at the progress we have made and find that half the work is already done, it is just possible that our faith will have become so strong that we can move all the rest at once.

1 Mt. 17, 20.

Izvor Collection

201 – Toward a Solar Civilization
It is not enough to be familiar with the astronomical theory of heliocentricity. Since the sun is the centre of our universe, we must learn to put it at the centre of all our preoccupations and activities.

202 – Man, Master of His Destiny
If human beings are to be masters of their own destiny, they must understand that the laws which govern their physical, psychic and spiritual life are akin to those which govern the universe.

203 – Education Begins Before Birth
Humanity will improve and be transformed only when people realize the true import of the act of conception. In this respect, men and women have a tremendous responsibility for which they need years of preparation.

204 – The Yoga of Nutrition
The way we eat is as important as what we eat. Through our thoughts and feelings, it is possible to extract from our food spiritual elements which can contribute to the full flowering of our being.

205 – Sexual Force or the Winged Dragon
How to master, domesticate and give direction to our sexual energy so as to soar to the highest spheres of the spirit.

206 – A Philosophy of Universality
We must learn to replace our restricted, self-centred point of view with one that is immensely broad and universal. If we do this we shall all benefit; not only materially but particularly on the level of consciousness.

207 – What is a Spiritual Master
A true spiritual Master is, first, one who is conscious of the essential truths written by cosmic intelligence into the great book of Nature. Secondly, he must have achieved complete mastery of the elements of his own being. Finally, all the knowledge and authority he has acquired must serve only to manifest the qualities and virtues of selfless love.

208 – Under the Dove, the Reign of Peace
Peace will finally reign in the world only when human beings work to establish peace within themselves, in their every thought, feeling and action.

209 – Christmas and Easter in the Initiatic Tradition
Human beings are an integral part of the cosmos and intimately concerned by the process of gestation and birth going on in nature. Christmas and Easter – rebirth and resurrection – are simply two ways of envisaging humanity's regeneration and entry into the spiritual life.

210 – The Tree of the Knowledge of Good and Evil
Methods, not explanations, are the only valid answers to the problem of evil. Evil is an inner and outer reality which confronts us every day, and we must learn to deal with it.

211 – Freedom, the Spirit Triumphant
A human being is a spirit, a spark sprung from within the Almighty. Once a person understands, sees and feels this truth, he will be free.

212 – Light is a Living Spirit
Light, the living matter of the universe, is protection, nourishment and an agency for knowledge for human beings. Above all, it is the only truly effective means of self-transformation.

213 – Man's Two Natures, Human and Divine
Man is that ambiguous creature that evolution has placed on the borderline between the animal world and the divine world. His nature is ambivalent, and it is this ambivalence that he must understand and overcome.

214 – Hope for the World: Spiritual Galvanoplasty
On every level of the universe, the masculine and feminine principles reproduce the activity of those two great cosmic principles known as the Heavenly Father and the Divine Mother of which every manifestation of nature and life are a reflection. Spiritual galvanoplasty is a way of applying the science of these two fundamental principles to one's inner life.

215 – The True Meaning of Christ's Teaching
Jesus incorporated into the Our Father – or Lord's Prayer – an ancient body of knowledge handed down by Tradition and which had existed long before his time. A vast universe is revealed to one who knows how to interpret each of the requests formulated in this prayer.

216 – The Living Book of Nature
Everything in nature is alive and it is up to us to learn how to establish a conscious relationship with creation so as to receive that life within ourselves.

217 – New Light on the Gospels
The Parables and other tales from the Gospels are here interpreted as situations and events applicable to our own inner life.

218 – The Symbolic Language of Geometrical Figures
Each geometrical figure – circle, triangle, pentagram, pyramid or cross – is seen as a structure fundamental to the organization of the macrocosm (the universe) and the microcosm (human beings).

219 – Man's Subtle Bodies and Centres
However highly developed our sense organs, their scope will never reach beyond the physical plane. To experience richer and subtler sensations, human beings must exercise the subtler organs and spiritual centres that they also possess: the aura, the solar plexus, the Hara centre, the Chakras, and so on.

220 – The Zodiac, Key to Man and to the Universe
Those who are conscious of being part of the universe feel the need to work inwardly in order to find within themselves the fullness of the cosmic order so perfectly symbolized by the Zodiac.

221 – True Alchemy or The Quest for Perfection
Instead of fighting our weaknesses and vices – we would inevitably be defeated – we must learn to make them work for us. We think it normal to harness the untamed forces of nature, so why be surprised when a Master, an initiate, speaks of harnessing the primitive forces within us? This is true spiritual alchemy.

222 – Man's Psychic Life: Elements and Structures
"Know thyself" How to interpret this precept carved over the entrance to the temple at Delphi? To know oneself is to be conscious of one's different bodies, from the denser to the most subtle, of the principles which animate these bodies, of the needs they induce in one, and of the state of consciousness which corresponds to each.

223 – Creation: Artistic and Spiritual
Everyone needs to create but true creation involves spiritual elements. Artists, like those who seek the spirit, have to reach beyond themselves in order to receive elements from the higher planes.

224 – The Powers of Thought
Thought is a power, an instrument given to us by God so that we may become creators like himself – creators in beauty and perfection. This means that we must be extremely watchful, constantly verifying that what we do with our thoughts is truly for our own good and that of the whole world. This is the one thing that matters.

225 – Harmony and Health

Illness is a result of some physical or psychic disorder. The best defence against illness, therefore, is harmony. Day and night we must take care to be attuned and in harmony with life as a whole, with the boundless life of the cosmos.

226 – The Book of Divine Magic

True, divine magic, consists in never using the faculties, knowledge, or powers one has acquired for one's own self-interest, but always and only for the establishment of God's kingdom on earth.

227 – Golden Rules for Everyday Life

Why spoil one's life by chasing after things that matter less than life itself? Those who learn to give priority to life, who protect and preserve it in all integrity, will find more and more that they obtain their desires. For it is this, an enlightened, luminous life that can give them everything.

228 – Looking into the Invisible

Meditation, dreams, visions, astral projection all give us access to the invisible world, but the quality of the revelations received depends on our efforts to elevate and refine our perceptions.

229 – The Path of Silence

In every spiritual teaching, practices such as meditation and prayer have only one purpose: to lessen the importance attributed to one's lower nature and give one's divine nature more and more scope for expression. Only in this way can a human being experience true silence.

230 – The Book of Revelations: A Commentary

If *Revelations* is a difficult book to interpret it is because we try to identify the people, places and events it describes instead of concentrating on the essence of its message: a description of the elements and processes of our spiritual life in relation to the life of the cosmos.

231 – The Seeds of Happiness

Happiness is like a talent which has to be cultivated. Those who want to possess happiness must go in search of the elements which will enable them to nourish it inwardly; elements which belong to the divine world.

232 – The Mysteries of Fire and Water

Our psychic life is fashioned every day by the forces we allow to enter us, the influences that impregnate us. What could be more poetic, more meaningful than water and fire and the different forms under which they appear?

233 – Youth: Creators of the Future

Youth is full of life, enthusiasms and aspirations of every kind. The great question is how to channel its extraordinary, overflowing effervescence of energies.

234 – Truth, Fruit of Wisdom and Love

We all abide by our own "truth", and it is in the name of their personal "truth" that human beings are continually in conflict. Only those who possess true love and true wisdom discover the same truth and speak the same language.

235 – In Spirit and in Truth

Since we live on earth we are obliged to give material form to our religious beliefs. Sacred places and objects, rites, prayers and ceremonies are expressions of those beliefs. It is important to understand that they are no more than expressions – expressions which are always more or less inadequate. They are not themselves the religion, for religion exists in spirit and in truth.

236 – Angels and Other Mysteries of the Tree of Life

God is like a pure current of electricity which can reach us only through a series of transformers. These transformers are the countless luminous beings which inhabit the heavens and which tradition calls the Angelic Hierarchies. It is through them that we receive divine life; through them that we are in contact with God.

237 – Cosmic Balance, the Secret of Polarity

Libra – the Scales – symbolizes cosmic balance, the equilibrium of the two opposite and complementary forces, the masculine and feminine principles, by means of which the universe came into being and continues to exist. The symbolism of Libra, expression of this twofold polarity, dominates the whole of creation.

238 – The Faith That Moves Mountains

Faith is the result of an age-old knowledge buried deep within our subconscious. It is founded on an experience of the divine world, an experience which has left indelible traces on each one of us and which we must reanimate.

By the same author

(translated from the French)

"Complete Works" Collection

Brochures:

New Presentation

Live Recordings on Tape

KC2510An — The Laws of Reincarnation
(Two audio cassettes)

(available in French only)

K 2001 Fr — La science de l'unité
K 2002 Fr — Le bonheur
K 2003 Fr — La vraie beauté
K 2004 Fr — L'éternel printemps
K 2005 Fr — La loi de l'enregistrement
K 2006 Fr — La science de l'éducation
K 2007 Fr — La prière
K 2008 Fr — L'esprit et la matière
K 2009 Fr — Le monde des archétypes
K 2010 Fr — L'importance de l'ambiance
K 2011 Fr — Le yoga de la nutrition
K 2012 Fr — L'aura
K 2013 Fr — Déterminisme et indéterminisme
K 2014 Fr — Les deux natures de l'être humain
K 2015 Fr — Prendre et donner
K 2016 Fr — La véritable vie spirituelle
K 2017 Fr — La mission de l'art
K 2018 Fr — Il faut laisser l'amour véritable se manifester
K 2019 Fr — Comment orienter la force sexuelle
K 2020 Fr — Un haut idéal pour la jeunesse
K 2021 Fr — La réincarnation - Preuves de la réincarnation
dans les Évangiles.
K 2022 Fr — La réincarnation - Rien ne se produit par hasard,
une intelligence préside à tout.
K 2023 Fr — La réincarnation - L'aura et la réincarnation.
K 2024 Fr — La loi de la responsabilité
K 2551 Fr — La réincarnation (coffret de 3 cassettes)
K 2552 Fr — Introduction à l'astrologie initiatique
(coffret de 3 cassettes)
K 2553 Fr — La méditation (coffret de 3 cassettes)

Publisher-Distributor
Editions PROSVETA S.A. – B.P. 12 – F - 83601 Fréjus Cedex (France)
Tel. (00 33) 04 94 40 82 41 - Fax (00 33) 04 94 40 80 05
Web: **www.prosveta.com**
E-mail: **international@prosveta.com**

Distributors

AUSTRALIA
SURYOMA LTD – P.O. Box 798 – Brookvale – N.S.W. 2100
Tel. / Fax: (61) 2 9984 8500 – E-mail: info@suryoma.com

AUSTRIA
HARMONIEQUELL VERSAND – A-5302 Henndorf, Hof 37
Tel. / Fax: (43) 6214 7413 – E-mail: info@prosveta.at

BELGIUM
PROSVETA BENELUX – Liersesteenweg 154 B-2547 Lint
Tel.: (32) 3/455 41 75 – Fax: 3/454 24 25 – E-mail: prosveta@skynet.be
N.V. MAKLU Somersstraat 13-15 – B-2000 Antwerpen
Tel.: (32) 3/321 29 00 – Fax: 3/233 26 59
VANDER S.A. – Av. des Volontaires 321 – B-1150 Bruxelles
Tel.: (32) 27 62 98 04 – Fax: 27 62 06 62

BRAZIL
NOBEL SA – Rua da Balsa, 559 – CEP 02910 – São Paulo, SP

BULGARIA
SVETOGLED – Bd Saborny 16 A, appt 11 – 9000 Varna
Tel. / Fax: (359) 52 23 98 02 – E-mail: svetgled@revolta.com

CANADA
PROSVETA Inc. – 3950, Albert Mines – North Hatley, QC J0B 2C0
Tel.: (1) 819 564-8212 – Fax: (1) 819 564-1823
In Canada, call toll free: 1-800-854-8212
E-mail: prosveta@prosveta-canada.com — www.prosveta-canada.com

COLUMBIA
PROSVETA – Avenida 46 n° 19-14 (Palermo) – Santafé de Bogotá
Tel.: (57) 232-01-36 – Fax: (57) 633-58-03

CYPRUS
THE SOLAR CIVILISATION BOOKSHOP
73 D Kallipoleos Avenue – Lycavitos – P.O. Box 4947, 1355 – Nicosia
Tel.: 02 377503 and 09 680854 – E-mail: pulper@dm.net.lb

CZECH REPUBLIC
PROSVETA Tchèque – Ant. Sovy 18 – České Budejovice 370 05
Tel. / Fax: (420) 38-53 00 227 – E-mail: prosveta@seznam.cz

GERMANY
PROSVETA Deutschland – Postfach 16 52 – 78616 Rottweil
Tel.: (49) 741-46551 – Fax: (49) 741-46552 – E-mail: prosveta.de@t-online.de
EDIS GmbH, Mühlweg 2 – 82054 Sauerlach
Tel.: (49) 8104-6677-0 – Fax: (49) 8104-6677-99

GREECE
PROSVETA – VAMVACAS INDUSTRIAL EQUIPEMENT
Moutsopoulou 103 – 18541 Piraeus

HAITI
P.O. Box 115 – Jacmel, Haiti (W.I.) – Tel. / Fax: (509) 288-3319

HOLLAND
STICHTING PROSVETA NEDERLAND
Zeestraat 50 – 2042 LC Zandvoort – E-mail: prosveta@worldonline.nl

HONG KONG
SWINDON BOOK CO LTD
246 Deck 2, Ocean Terminal – Harbour City – Tsimshatsui, Kowloon

IRELAND
PROSVETA – The Doves Nest, Duddleswell Uckfield – East Sussex TN 22 3JJ
Tel.: (44) (01825) 712988 – Fax: (44) (01825) 713386
E-mail: prosveta@pavilion.co.uk

ISRAEL
GAL ATAIA – 58 Bar-Kohva street – Tel-Aviv
Tel.: 00 972 3 5286264 – Fax: 00 972 3 5286260

ITALY
PROSVETA Coop. – Casella Postale – 06060 Moiano (PG)
Tel. / Fax: (39) 075-8358498 – E-mail: prosveta@tin.it

LUXEMBOURG
PROSVETA BENELUX – Liersesteenweg 154 B-2547 Lint

NORWAY
PROSVETA NORDEN – Postboks 5101 – 1503 Moss
Tel.: 69 26 51 40 – Fax: 69 25 06 76
E-mail: prosveta Norden – prosnor@online.no

PORTUGAL
EDIÇÕE PROSVETA – Rua Passos Manuel, n° 20 – 3° E, P 1150 – Lisboa
Tel.: (351) (21) 354 07 64
PUBLICAÇÕES EUROPA-AMERICA Ltd
Est Lisboa-Sintra KM 14 – 2726 Mem Martins Codex

ROMANIA
ANTAR – Str. N. Constantinescu 10 – Bloc 16A – sc A – Apt. 9
Sector 1 – 71253 Bucarest – Tel.: (40) 1 679 52 48 – Tel. / Fax: (40) 1 231 37 19

RUSSIA
S. Neapolitensky: 40 Gorohovaya – Appt 1 – Saint-Petersbourg
Tel.: (70) 812 5327 184 / (70) 812 2726 876 – Fax: (70) 812 1582 363
E. Jitniouk: Pr. Vernadskogo, d. 66, kv. 15 – Moscou 117 454

SINGAPORE & MALAYSIA
AMERICASIA GLOBAL MARKETING – Clementi Central Post Office
P.O. Box 108 – Singapore 911204
Tel.: (65) 892 0503 – Fax: (65) 95 199 198
E-mail: harvard1@mbox4.singnet.com.sg

SPAIN
ASOCIACIÓN PROSVETA ESPAÑOLA
C/ Ausias March n° 23 Ático – SP-08010 Barcelona
Tel.: (34) (3) 412 31 85 – Fax: (34) (3) 302 13 72
E-mail: aprosveta@prosveta.es

SWITZERLAND
PROSVETA Société Coopérative – CH – 1808 Les Monts-de-Corsier
Tel.: (41) 21 921 92 18 – Fax: (41) 21 922 92 04
E-mail: prosveta@swissonline.ch

UNITED KINGDOM
PROSVETA – The Doves Nest, Duddleswell Uckfield – East Sussex TN 22 3JJ
Tel.: (44) (01825) 712988 – Fax: (44) (01825) 713386
E-mail: prosveta@pavilion.co.uk

UNITED STATES
PROSVETA U.S.A. – P.O. Box 1176 – New Smyrna Beach, FL 32170-1176
Tel. / Fax: (904) 428-1465
E-mail: sales@prosveta-usa.com — www.prosveta-usa.com

VENEZUELA
BETTY MUÑÕZ – Calle Madrid – Quinta Lydia – Las Mercedes – D. F. Caracas